EDITORIAL

Piet Lombaerde
Editor in chief
–

This issue of the ADS-cahier (from now on named *Antwerp Design Sciences*) is celebrating its 10th anniversary. It has a special theme: current doctoral theses at the Associated Faculty of Design Sciences of the Antwerp University College (AUHA).

These doctorates involve young post-graduates of the department as well as associate professors who are connected to the Associated Faculty of Design Sciences. Many of these doctorates in preparation will be defended at Antwerp University, but a limited number at other national and international universities as well. Regarding individual specialties and the selected subjects, there is a constant striving for collaboration between our programmes and the most suitable corresponding or supplementary departments. After all, many of the subjects dealt with in the fields of architecture- and product development, demand an interdisciplinary approach which can only improve the quality of these doctorate theses.

To give a clear overview of all these future doctorates, the subjects covered have been arranged in groups or sections.
They describe a wide range of research areas which are currently present in the Design Sciences department and the various units and study groups.

An initial section deals with 'Integrated Product Development and Design', in which specific subjects are covered, like sustainable design in relation to management (**Elli Verhulst**), performance and innovation (**Alexis Jacoby**), a new method of transplant with better mechanical properties as prosthesis or arthrodesis (**Theo Linders**), and the study of design guidelines and recommendations for the development of non-stigmatising, bodily-near products (**Kristof Vaes**).

A second section deals with 'Constructive, Technical and Digital Research Studies in Architecture'. For example, **Stijn Verbeke** does research into thermal comfort and thermal inertia. **Saskia Gabriël's** studies include the problem of assessing daylight and fire safety in the design of atriums. Sustainability in Group Housing is the subject of **Bart Janssens'** doctorate. **Kathleen De Bodt's** subject is Design Methodology.

Several units and study groups are involved in Research Studies in Human Sciences and Urban Planning. Town Planning and Urbanism are well represented in the doctorates that deal with the dialectics between urbanicity and creative agency (**Koenraad Keignaert**), the search for qualitative methods to involve social analysis in spatial planning (**Katrijn Apostel**), research into the lifestyle in housing requirements in Flanders (**Ann Pisman**), and research into spatial quality in strategic projects (**Marleen Goethals**). Another study focuses on the role of Landscape Planning in urban networks (**David Verhoestraete**).

Another important segment of research is that of Architectural History and Cultural Studies. Once again several study groups and units are involved in this scientific research. It is also typical that some subjects create a relationship between various units, which then generates new opportunities from a didactic point of view. Moreover, this section of research comprises both fundamental and basic research, as well as applied and *research by design*.
An important segment includes architectural history and research into the history of urban development.
Jochen De Vylder is researching the origins of the early modern city design in a number of towns in the Northern and Southern Netherlands around 1600. Using digital analyses, **Nathalie Poppe** is analysing the specific role and significance of light

in Baroque churches in Europe (17th century) by using digital software programmes. **Els Van Hamme** is questioning the possible innovations in construction, technology and materials in Jesuit churches in the Low Countries.

As far as the 19th century is concerned, **Katrien Hebbelinck** is doing post-graduate research into the work of Eduard Keilig, a pioneer of park- and garden architecture in Belgium. **Pieter Brosens** is working on a doctoral thesis on the architecture and urbanism of father and son Van Steenbergen, stressing the evolution of two generations of architects during the second half of the 20th century in Antwerp. **Eva Storgaard**'s doctoral thesis analyses the architecture of dwelling in Belgium during the high conjuncture period 1958-1973.

This group of doctoral studies also includes two more post-graduate studies with an emphasis on culture: **Koen Van Synghel** is working on the critical architectural dimension in the plastic arts, and **Sigrid Van der Auwera** is researching how cultural property can be protected from destruction during armed conflicts. There is also a specific doctoral thesis by **Inge Somers** on theory of Interior Architecture in Flanders, framed in an international context.

As we have said, as far as the type of research is concerned, fundamental or basic research as well as applied, generic or *research by design* will be dealt with. Our aim is to create a balance between these three kinds of research. *Research by design* is quite new to scientific research. It closely resembles practice and the design process which is also its breeding ground. Consequently, this kind of research is not only closely linked to actual issues connected to architecture, interior design, urban planning, the preservation of monuments and historic buildings and the product development, but also draws inspiration from it. The proposed research hypotheses are based on the pragmatism of modern realism and on a scientific idiom of action. The design attempts to find an answer to this highly specific issue, and the way in which the design process is described, analytically, critically, and synthetically is the essence of this method of doctoral research. It is fairly new within the wide range of academic research. Consequently, there must be a clear indication of the demarcation criteria for new research, particularly with regard to its scientific value. After all, there is a danger that research based on social services is automatically labelled design research. The relationship between design and research in the Design Sciences is new when it comes to striving for quality in the academic world. Indeed, in our department we are eagerly awaiting the first doctorates to be produced which originate in design.

The number of doctorate studies that have been started in the Department of Design Sciences is rather large, which also means that there is a huge dynamism among young graduates and a number of professors to further explore the material they have studied and taking it to the level of doctoral research. It is therefore most opportune that the University College has created an academic budget for research. Moreover, the so-called BOF (*Bijzondere Onderzoeks Fondsen* - Special Research Funds) grants may be used. They can sometimes lead up to develop research themes that may be converted into post-graduate research in a subsequent phase. In a limited number of cases, candidates may also use the so-called Dehousse-funds, which provides them with a full researcher status over a period of four years. One possibility that has been insufficiently exploited up to now is the registrarship, of which up to 50% may be used for post-graduate research. ■

THE HUMAN SIDE OF SUSTAINABLE DESIGN FROM THE PERSPECTIVE OF CHANGE MANAGEMENT

Elli Verhulst
Artesis University College of Antwerp
elli.verhulst@artesis.be
–

Sustainable design is steadily becoming a well-known concept within the field of product innovation. Despite several drivers that support sustainability in design, a gap is described in literature between the theoretical foundations of sustainable design and its industrial implementation. In this doctoral research project, the influence of human factors on the implementation of sustainable design criteria in product innovation businesses is the subject of study. A literature review and a preliminary research have led to the development of a conceptual model that aims to explain the role of human factors in sustainable design implementation. Several case studies will be performed in order to verify and improve this model.

KEYWORDS
Sustainable design implementation, change management, human factors

INTRODUCTION
Several drivers such as depletion of resources, rising prices of raw materials and energy prices, novel international regulations on environmental and social issues, etc., account for the growing awareness of sustainability within governments, the market and businesses. Companies that develop, produce and commercialise innovative products have a prominent role in the incorporation of sustainability in the product development process. In order to implement sustainability criteria in industrial design, several tools and methods are available (Tischner and Charter, 2001). However, literature has described a gap between the theoretical foundations of sustainable design and the industrial implementation thereof (Tukker et al., 2001; Baumann et al., 2002; Mc Aloone et al., 2002).

Recent research has observed and identified several success factors and obstacles for this type of integration process. These include factors which are closely related to the structure of the organisation and factors which are more linked to personal and emotional aspects. Only few studies emphasise the importance of these human aspects in sustainable design (Boks, 2006; Cohen-Rosenthal, 2000). However, in adjacent fields such as change management, this 'human side' of the integration process is considered as an important issue. Considering the aim to assure an acceptable success rate of this sort of implementation processes, scientific knowledge from this adjoining discipline can offer new insights on the subject.

The goal of this research is to find out how and to which extent knowledge on change management can support and improve the implementation process of sustainable design criteria in design businesses. In order to answer this main question, three research questions are postulated:

RQ 1: How does an implementation process of sustainable design criteria differentiate itself from a generic change process?

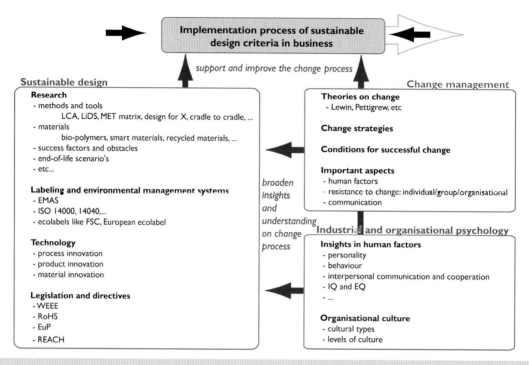

RQ 2: How do internal and external factors affect the implementation process of sustainable design criteria in business?

RQ3: How is the implementation process of sustainability criteria related to the product development process?

In addition to gathering more profound insights on the integration process of sustainable design criteria, this research may ultimately lead to prescriptive insights for successful implementation of sustainable design criteria and offer practical guidelines to companies that are in an initial stage of such a challenging process.

CONTENT AND SUBJECT

A literature review on product development, sustainable design and change management was carried out. In this literature review, possible influencing factors on change processes have been gathered and interpreted in the case of sustainable design implementation.

As a result, four propositions have been formulated out of these critical success factors which combine the knowledge from the research fields of organisational change and development with the area of sustainable design in business.

A second step in the research was a qualitative, preliminary research. Interviews were conducted within companies that have experience with the first stages of the implementation process of sustainability criteria in design, in order to test the validity of the propositions. Alongside this verification, we investigated and monitored a number of factors that differentiate the implementation process of sustainable design criteria from more generic organisational changes.

Following the results of this preliminary research, a conceptual model has been proposed, as shown in Figure 2. This model combines theoretical input from the literature review with empirical evidence from the work field. Information is thereby assimilated on the new product development process, different steps that should be taken to incorporate sustainability criteria into the product development process, the consecutive stages of a change process, and the role of influencing human factors on these processes related to timing within.

The conceptual model serves as a starting point for the accomplishment of several case studies. On the one hand, the model serves as guidance for keeping the focus of the case study research on the aspects mentioned in the model. On the other hand, it provides a theoretical concept of an implementation process of sustainable design criteria that will be explored and enriched, and whose added value will be verified in practice.

RESULTS AND DISCUSSION

Both the literature study and the preliminary study offer a number of interesting insights in the way knowledge from the field of change management might support the implementation of sustainable design criteria in business. Moreover, some generic and specific factors clearly show the discerning elements between a general change process and the implementation process of sustainable design criteria. The most relevant factors that emerged from both the literature and the work field are: the added value of the changes that will be introduced, the knowledge to be learned on sustainable design issues and the culture that is needed in order to successfully implement the changes.

However, the preliminary qualitative study was accomplished within a limited number of companies and therefore the results cannot be generalised to all design industries. Further research in the form of case studies will be conducted in the coming months in a broader scope, with the aim to strengthen or correct the current insights.

CONCLUSION

Based on the existing literature and empirical evidence found in practice, it can be stated that the implementation process of

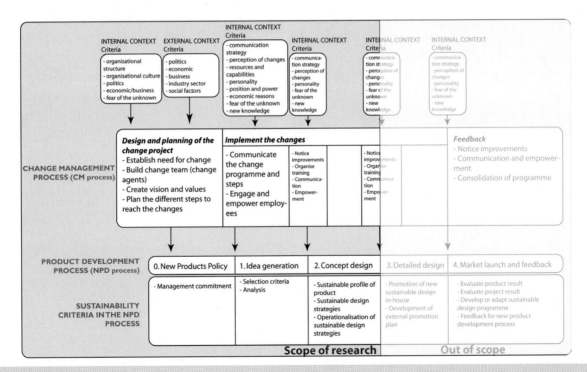

CONCEPTUAL MODEL EXPLAINING THE ROLE OF HUMAN FACTORS IN SUSTAINABLE DESIGN IMPLEMENTATION

sustainable design criteria in design businesses can indeed be supported and improved by knowledge on change management. The formulation of a clear added value of sustainability in design, offering educational programmes on the subject and incorporating a culture that is open to sustainability issues might already improve this integration process. However, more profound evidence should be gathered by performing several case studies in order to endorse the current findings.

As a conclusion, the present and supplementary insights of this research might lead companies to support their own implementation process of sustainability criteria in design with additional but indispensable knowledge on organisational change, thereby guiding them towards successful and sustainable change. ■

Ph.D Thesis Directors
Prof. dr. ir. Henri Masson
Prof. dr. Casper Boks

REFERENCES

Baumann, H., Boons, F., Bragd, A. Mapping the green product development field: engineering, policy and business perspectives, pp. 409-425 *Journal of Cleaner Production* 10. 2002.

Boks, C. The Soft Side of Ecodesign. *Journal of Cleaner Production*, 14: 1346-1356. 2006.

Cohen-Rosenthal, E. A walk on the human side of industrial ecology, *American Behaviour Scientist*, Vol. 44 No. 2: 245-264. 2000.

McAloone, T., Bey, N., Boks, C., Ernzer, M., Wimmer, W. Towards The Actual Implementation of Ecodesign in Industry - The Haves and Needs viewed by the European Ecodesign Community. *Proceedings of CARE Innovation 2002, November 25-28, Vienna, Austria. 2002.*

Tischner, U. and Charter, M. *Sustainable Solutions - Developing Products and Services for the Future*. Greenleaf Publishing Ltd. Sheffield, UK. 2001.

Tukker, A. et al. Eco-design: The State of Implementation in Europe. pp. 147-161 *The Journal of Sustainable Product Design*. Vol. 1. 2001.

PERFORMANCE IN THE FRONT-END OF INNOVATION

ADS
19/20

Alexis Jacoby
Artesis University College of Antwerp
alexis.jacoby@artesis.be
–

Many factors are known to have a positive or negative impact on proficiency in front-end activities. Some of these aspects are strategic; others have a contextual or methodological nature. From a methodological point of view, the main issue is to find a way through the fuzzy process of front-end in order to deliver a result at the end of the process with some guarantee of success.

This research focuses on the process and deliverables of product definition to increase performance in the front-end of innovation. The main research topic is to find out in what way the product definition process can contribute to a successful approach in the front-end of innovation.

KEYWORDS

Front-end of innovation, methodology, idea generation, product definition, innovation strategy

INTRODUCTION

Innovation projects in industries are generally divided into three major areas: The Front-End of Innovation (FEI), The New Products Development (NPD) and the Product Launch or commercialization. Koen et al. (2001) among others define FEI activities as the activities that come before the more formal and well-structured activities of the New Product Development. FEI activities are less structured, less predictable than the formal stage-gate processes, used in NPD. Kim & Wilemon (2002) define FEI as 'the period between when an opportunity is first considered and when an idea is judged ready for development'.

There is no discussion about the importance of innovation, or about the importance of the front-end activities in the overall innovation cycle. Cooper (1993) found that predevelopment

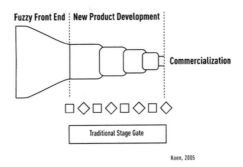

THE INNOVATION PROCESS: KOEN, (2005)

work has a positive impact on reducing development time and improving the success rate. Koen et al (2001) argued that highly innovative companies are proficient in front-end activities.

The need for innovation drives many companies to seek for strategy, methodology, tools and techniques to support this early stage product development

Although a lot of literature is written on this subject, innovation in general consists of high-risk activities of which the outcome is uncertain and often unpredictable. Every day, practitioners in innovative industries are confronted with practical and strategic problems to get innovative projects running and to guarantee some kind of success at the end of the road. Many people with very different backgrounds are involved in the process and it is a challenge to steer the entire organization in the right direction, to reach a successful business target.

Prior research has detected many business-related or external factors that are linked to success or failure in Innovation. On top of that, a lot of supporting methods and tools are specified by consultants and researchers. And yet, it is often unclear how to proceed in the pre-development phases of innovation projects.

8

Some people refer to these activities as the fuzzy front-end.
This research aims to gain more insight into the 'front-end of innovation'. The particular point of view on the issue is the way a product definition is defined and changed throughout the front-end activities.
Due to the fact that front-end innovation processes are often regarded from the business point of view, previous research has never enlightened the role product definition can play in this difficult and yet so important part of new product development.

CONTENT AND SUBJECT

The preliminary desk research has focused on the known success factors in the front-end of innovation and the tools and methodologies known to the scientific world. The process has been divided into its different subphases in order to understand the rationale and specificities of each of these different subphases.
In a second phase, all known elements of product definition throughout the front-end have been reviewed and brought together.
This desk research has resulted in a framework that covers the front-end of innovation (Figure 2).

As a result, a review was proposed on this issue with all known elements inside.
During the empirical part of the research (2008-2009) several innovation projects will be examined in innovation minded companies through interviews with different stakeholders in a front-end project. This multiple case study will collect data on the output and the quality of the output at every subphase in the front-end of innovation. There will be a specific focus, however, on the interface between the strategic and operational level of the front-end activities.
The data collection through semi-structured interviews will be supported by documents research on final or provisional product and project definitions.

The variables to be looked into are, among others, the different process steps, the process owners, the input and output of the process steps, the quality of the output, the control on the results and the degree of detail in the results.

RESULTS AND DISCUSSION

This doctoral research must come to a conclusion at the end of 2010.
By then, the research should have reached a theoretical and a practical objective: the knowledge on the front-end of innovation should be extended with a more detailed view on the way a product definition should evolve during the front-end of innovation.
Secondly, based on the results, it should be possible to define guidelines that can help practitioners in their daily struggle to define future business ideas, in order to obtain more efficiency and effectiveness in their own process of front-end activities.

CONCLUSION

The theoretical part of this research is to be followed by the empirical part. Throughout the coming year, 30 to 50 interviews will be conducted of which the data will be analysed on a wide range of variables.
The results will provide an insight into the functions that product definition can have in the process of product innovation and which aspects of product definition need further attention. ■

Ph.D Thesis Directors
Prof. dr. Johan Braet (UA)
Prof. Paul Verhaert
Artesis University College of Antwerp
Prof. dr. Jan Buijs
TU Delft

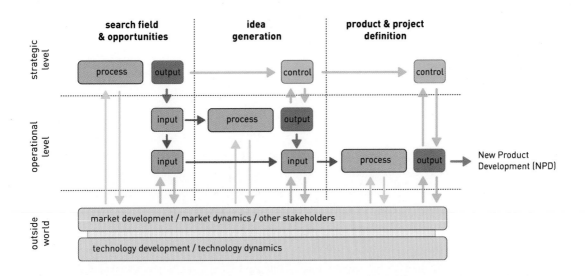

REFERENCES

Afuah Allan (2003): **Innovation Management**, Oxford University Press Inc., USA.

Braet J, Verhaert P (2007): **The practice of new products and new business**, uitgeverij ACCO, Leuven.

Buijs J, Valkenburg Rianne (2005): **Integrale Productontwikkeling**, Lemma, Utrecht.

Cooper R G, Kleinschmidt E J (1993): **Major New Products: what distinguishes the Winners in the Chemical Industry**, The journal of Product Innovation Management, 10; 90-111.

Crawford C M, Di Benedetto C A (2006): **New Products Management**, 8th edition, MCGraw-Hill/Irwin, New York.

Kim J, Wilemon D (2002): **Strategic issues in managing innovation's fuzzy front-end**, European Journal of Innovation Management, vol 5, 2002, 27-39t.

Koen et al. (2001): **Providing clarity and a common language to the "Fuzzy Front End"?** Research - Technology Management, 44 (2): 46-55

Sandmeier P, Jamali N, Kobe C, Enkel E, Gassmann O, Meier M (2004): **Towards a structured and integrative Front-end of product innovation**, conference paper, R&D management Conference, (RADMA), Lissabon, Portugal.

Trott P (2002): **Innovation Management and New Product Development**, Prentice Hall, Pearson education, Harlow, England.

Wilson E (1994): **Improving Market Success Rates through Better Product Definition**, World class design to manufacture, Volume 1, Number 4; pp. 13-15(3).

THE CONSTRAINED KNEE, A NEW APPROACH

Theo Linders
Delft University of Technology Dept. of Industrial Design Engineering
Artesis University College of Antwerp
theo.linders@artesis.be
—

The current hinged knee has several shortcomings e.g. loosening and a very short lifespan, 10 years or less are no exception. After the failure of the prosthesis, in most cases, the surgeon's only solution is arthrodesis. The aim of this study is to identify the mechanisms that have a negative impact on this prosthesis and to design a new transplant with better mechanical properties, while maintaining or even increasing the freedom of movement for the patient, but most important of all, to obtain a longer lifespan.

KEYWORDS
Total knee arthroplasty, TKA, constrained knee, hinged knee, biomaterials, chronic knee instability, bone cancer.

INTRODUCTION
The Ph.D deals with a research project concerning a constrained knee prosthesis which is used for people with severe knee instability, bone cancer, heavy arthrosis or who have suffered a huge knee trauma. The main reason I chose this subject is that I will need this kind of surgery myself within a few years.

The main question in this research is to find out whether a TKA with a better biomechanical mechanism in combination with new materials and coating, can have an impact on the lifespan and therefore on the patient's contentment.

I am still in the first stage of my Ph.D where I am studying the different publications and books. This involves a study of the history of the TKA, finding out the reasons why some types were not successful, determining the costs for this prosthesis and the effects on health insurance when its life can be prolonged.

CONTENT AND SUBJECT
Starting with a literature study, a summary is made of all currently used hinged knees with their pros and contras, the medical reasons why this surgery is used, the history of the TKA and the financial impact on patient and health insurance.

This will be followed by a patient research in a 4 or 5 Western European countries concerning contentment and functional possibilities.

Next, a study will be made about all the mechanical and physical reasons which lead to the final failure of the prosthesis. Influences of food, medication, every day activities will be considered. From this research a list of demands will be extracted, covering the surgeon's needs and the patient's wishes.

Research will be done on new materials for the prosthesis itself, but also, and perhaps even more importantly, for the coatings to be used in order to obtain better fixation in the bone and less rejection of the metallic parts by the human body.

In the final part of the Ph.D, a new design will be made taking into account all the research results. Finite element calculations for strength, wear and tear and kinematic analysis will be made, followed by a physical verification in the laboratory. Tooling for the operation will be reviewed and reused where possible. Finally, an economical study of the new prosthesis will be made.

RESULTS AND DISCUSSION

Because most companies active in this field spend the greater part of their research budget on "common" TKA, there still remains a lot to be done for this special product. Not much progress has been made to date on these prostheses. Admittedly, the use of some different materials has been studied, but functionally they have not progressed at all.

By designing a new hinge that copies the movement of the natural knee, it is hoped to obtain better results in the long run.

CONCLUSION

It is too early to report any conclusions as I amjust in the initial phase of the Ph.D. In the second stage I will start with a research of patients who already have this kind of prosthesis, to find out what their experiences are, what the reasons were for this operation, what kind of TKA was placed, do they take medications, etc. The conclusions from this study will lead to a better understanding of the key factors involved. ■

Ph.D Thesis Directors
Dr.Johan Molenbroek
TU Delft, Faculty of Industrial Design Engineering,
Prof. Dr. Johan Bellemans,
UZ Leuven
Dr. Luc Labey, Smith & Nephew

ACKNOWLEDGEMENTS

I wish to thank, Prof. Dr Johan Bellemans, Dr. Luc Labey, and Dr. Johan Molenbroek.

REFERENCES

J.Bellemans, M.Ries, J.Victor (eds), *Total Knee Arthroplasty*, Heidelberg, 2005, pp.288-404.

G.Scuderi, A.Tria (eds), *Knee Arthroplasty Handbook*, New York, 2006, pp.70-103, pp.133-149.

J.Bono, R.Scott (eds), *Revision Total Knee Arthroplasty, New York, 2005, pp.219-236*

M.Nietert, Untersuchungen zur Kinematik des menschlichen Kniegelenkes im Hinblick auf ihre Approximation in der Prothetik, Berlin, 1975

C.Abicht, *Künstliche Kniegelenke nach dem Viergelenkprinzip,* Greifswald, 2005

S.Kurtz, *The UHMWPE Handbook*, San Diego, 2004

DESIGN GUIDELINES AND RECOMMENDATIONS WITHIN THE NEW PRODUCT DEVELOPMENT PROCESS FOR THE DEVELOPMENT OF NON-STIGMATISING, BODILY-NEAR PRODUCTS

Kristof Vaes
Artesis University College of Antwerp
kristof.vaes@artesis.be
–

CASE STUDY: THE PROTECTION OF ASTHMATIC CHILDREN AGAINST FINE DUST

The science of product development consists of research on and development of methodologies and strategies, that strive to augment the success of new products on the market. (Verhaert et al. 2006, Roozenburg en Eekels 1995, Pahl en Beitz 1996).

Not all products have the same chances and assets as they are launched. Apart from the 'popular' products, that give us the ability to express ourselves as consumers, there are those products that provide us with far less emotional benefits. One category of these products is intended to release us from discomforting or unsafe situations. A lot of these products are often stigmatizing, socially unaccepted, uncomfortable and are perceived by their users as unpleasant.

After analysing the factors that make these products stigmatizing and "unwanted", on the one hand. And on the other hand studying why other, more popular bodily-near products, are easily accepted by users, this study will investigate how the product designer can positively influence the acceptance of stigmatizing products. Verhaert et al. (2006) divide the product development process into the following consecutive phases, regardless of the discipline(s) on which they apply: problem and product definition, system design, product solutions and detailed design. The design recommendations that will be developed and tested will all be applicable in the early stage of the design process, being the problem and product definition. The deliverable of this study will be a framework for designers and design researchers that will enable them to increase the acceptance of stigmatizing, bodily-near products.

The usefulness will be validated by a case study: the development of an individual, efficient, socially accepted and child-friendly protection for asthmatic children against fine dust. The necessity of this product can be validated by the growing evidence of a causal relationship between ambient air pollution and asthma related symptoms (Desager et al.,2006; Farhat et al., 2005; Ward et al., 2004; Masoli et al., 2004; Ha et al., 2003; Wickman et al., 2003; Pope et al., 2002; von Klot et al., 2002; Burnett et al., 2001; Schwartz et al., 2001; Dockery and Pope, 1992).

KEYWORDS

pleasurable products, design research, collaborative research strategies, usability, social stigma, fine dust

INTRODUCTION

This doctoral thesis started in January 2008 as a result of a preliminary collaboration between the University of Antwerp's Environmental Analysis Group, the University of Antwerp's Hospital Paediatrics, and the University College of Antwerp's Product Development. supported by the Special Research Funding of the Association of Antwerp (BOF), The aim of this preliminary study was to investigate the specifications that could lead to the development of a new personal protection for children that should remove fine dust from the inhaled air, and thus reduce the asthma prevalence in children during high air pollution episodes. The output consisted of an inventory of all requirements and desires of future users and experts, and a multidisciplinary translation hereof to specified and well-founded product specifications.

Methodological research in product development has shown that an extensive and profound preliminary study of economical, scientific/technological and social sciences increases the chance to create a successful product and reduces the duration of a product development process (Koen et al., 2002).

For the doctoral thesis the emphasis has been placed on the social acceptance, user-friendliness and pleasurability of all stigmatising, bodily near products. This research aims to scan several research domains, like paediatrics, psychology, sociology, marketing and product design in search for valuable research strategies that could serve as inspiration for a design tool that can help designers in making unwanted products more accepted and pleasurable.

CONTENT AND SUBJECT

The following chapters outline some of the topics that are currently being studied in the first phase of the literature research. A more precise research question and strategy will be defined in the next months.

PLEASURE-BASED APPROACHES

These days, industrial design departments within most major companies and design consultancies employ a number of specialists charged with ensuring that product designs fit the needs of those who will use the products. In many product areas, technical advances and manufacturing processes have reached a level of sophistication that makes any potential competitive advantage, in terms of functionality, reliability and manufacturing costs, marginal. Many manufacturers now consider *design* as one of the few areas in which it is still possible to gain significant advantages over the competition. Good human factors are, of course, central to achieving excellence in design.

Customers have come to expect products to be easy to use, usability has moved from being what marketing professionals call a 'satisfier' to being a 'dissatisfier'. In other words, people are no longer pleasantly surprised when a product is useable, but are unpleasantly surprised by difficulty in use.

But still, these usability-based approaches are limited because they tend to look at products as tools with which users complete tasks. However, products are not merely tools: they can be seen as living objects with which people have relationships. Products are objects that can make people happy or angry, proud or ashamed, secure or anxious. Products can empower, infuriate or delight - they have personality (Marzano 1998).

People also have personalities. Not only do they have personalities, but they also have hopes, fears, dreams and aspirations. These are liable to affect the way that people respond to and interact with products.

It is a rarity to find published human-factors studies that describe people in terms that go beyond factors such as age, gender, education or profession. Similarly, these studies only seem to be concerned with the level of effectiveness, efficiency and satisfaction with which people can perform tasks; not with their emotional responses to the products that they are using and experiencing.

The human-factors profession has traditionally operationalised 'satisfaction' in a manner that is limited to the avoidance of physical or cognitive discomfort.

Pleasure-based approaches to product design can be seen as approaches that consider all of the potential benefits that a product can deliver. It is important to note that pleasure with products accrues from the relationship between a person and a product. 'Pleasurability', then, is not simply a property of a product but of the interaction between a product and person.

In recent years, many researchers have focussed on emotion and pleasure theories:
- Don Norman's emotional design model
- Patrick Jordan's pleasure model
- McCarthy and Wright's Technology as Experience framework.

In the book of Patrick W. Jordan – Designing pleasurable products – a framework for addressing pleasure issues has been outlined. The author introduces four types of pleasure that could be derived from the interaction with a product.

- *Physio-pleasure*: It concerns the body and pleasures derived from the sensory organs. They include pleasures connected with touch, taste and smell as well as feelings of sensual pleasure.
- *Socio-pleasure:* This is the enjoyment derived from relationships with others. Products can, for example, facilitate social interaction.
- *Psycho-pleasure:* Psycho pleasure pertains to people's cognitive and emotional reactions. In the case of products, this might include issues relating to the cognitive demands of using the product and the emotional reactions engendered through experiencing the product.
- *Ideo-pleasure:* Ideo-pleasure pertains to people's values. These include, for example, tastes, moral values and personal aspirations. The issues that fall under ideological pleasure are important in defining how people do and would like to see themselves.

Once we have an understanding of the practical, emotional and hedonic benefits that a user wants to gain from a particular product, these benefits can be linked to the properties of the product design; and the design solutions can be evaluated to check if they can deliver the required benefits.

STIGMA

The desire to avoid stigma can be seen as a social need pleasure. Even more so, aside from helping to avoid social pitfalls, products can also contribute to creating positive social consequences – both for individuals and for society as a whole.

In the society, stigma is recognised as a powerful phenomenon with far-ranging effects on its targets (Crocker et al. 1998, Jones et al. 1984, Link & Phelan 2001). Stigma has been linked to poor mental health, physical illness, academic underachievement, low social status, poverty and reduced access to housing, education, and jobs.

Two articles serve as a starting point for this research:
- The social psychology of stigma (2005)
  Brenda Major and Laurie T. O'Brien
  Department of Psychology, University of California, Santa Barbara,
- A Dual-Process Model of Reactions to Perceived Stigma (2004)
  John B. Pryor, Glenn D. Reeder, Christopher Yeadon, and Matthew Hesson-McInnis
  Illinois State University

John B. Pryor (Ph.D., Professor of Psychology at Illinois State University) outlines a dual process of how people respond psychologically to someone who possesses a stigma. The heart of this theoretical model is the notion that psychological reactions at first encountered with someone who has a stigma have a predictable time course. A spontaneous or reflexive reaction may be followed by a delayed or thoughtful reaction.

In this research we will try to search and evaluate which products carry a stigmatising effect, and how this stigma affects the thoughts, feelings, behaviour, and health of its targets.

THE CASE STUDY: THE PROTECTION OF ASTHMATIC CHILDREN AGAINST FINE DUST.

In spite of various governmental efforts to reduce ambient air pollution in urban environments, citizens are being exposed to polluted air. Due to the growing evidence of a causal relationship between ambient air pollution and asthma related symptoms, an urgent solution is required. Since children are known to be the most susceptible population to air pollution, this research hopes to contribute to the development of an efficient, personal protection suitable for children, which they can wear during bike rides in the city e.g. at high air pollution episodes.

The protective device that has to be developed can be seen as a typical example of a stigmatising, 'bodily-near' product. We hope to validate our research by proving that our design recommendations and strategies provided a vital contribution to the 'usefulness' and 'pleasurability' of the product concept.

In this final phase of the research we hope to put our research strategy to the test and ask our target users (children between the ages of 5 and 12) to give their first-hand appreciation and feedback of existing or future conditions of the concept through active engagement with prototypes.
Apart from these experience prototypes we will search or develop efficient participatory and collaborative research strategies with children, so we can work with and extract knowledge and experience from children that's vital for us product designers and design researchers. ∎

Ph.D Thesis Directors
Prof. Dr. K. Desager
Pneumologie & Paediatrics, University Hospital Antwerp
Prof. Dr. P. J. Stappers
Technical University Delft, Faculty Industrial Design / Studiolab
Dr. M. Stranger (VITO)

REFERENCES

Braet J., Verhaert P., *The practice of new products and new business,* Acco, Leuven, 2007.

Buijs J., Valkenburg R.,*Integrale productontwikkeling,* 2de druk, Utrecht, 2002.

Burnett R.T., Smith-Doiron M., Stieb D., Raizenne M.E., Brook J.R., Dales R.E., Leech J.A., Cakmak S., Krewski D., *Association between ozone and hospitalisation for acute respiratory diseases in children less than 2 years of age,* American Journal of Epidemiology, 153(2001), 444-452

Crocker J., Major B., *Social stigma and self-esteem: the self-protective properties of stigma.*, Psychol. Rev. 96:608–30, 1989.

Desager K., *-Fijn stof: effecten op de respiratoire gezondheid van kinderen-* Congres van de Belgische Vereniging voor Kindergeneeskunde, 03-'06, Brugge

Green W.S., Jordan P. W., *Pleasure with Products: Beyond Usability*, CRC press, London, 2002

Ha E.H., Lee J.T., Kim H., Hong Y.C., et al., *Infant Susceptibility and mortality to air pollution in Seoul, South Korea, Pediatrics,* 111(2003), 284-290

Jones E.E., Farina A., Hastorf A.H., Markus H., Miller D.T., Scott R.A., *Social Stigma: The Psychology of Marked Relationships.*, New York, 1984

Jordan P. W., *Designing Pleasurable Products: An Introduction to the New Human Factors,* Taylor & Francis, London, 2000

Koen, P.A., Ajamian G.M., Boyce S., Clamen A., Fisher E., Fountoulakis S., Johnson A., Puri P., Seibert R., *Fuzzy-Front End: Effective Methods, Tools and Techniques,* 2002

Link B.G., Phelan J.C., *Conceptualizing stigma.*, Annu. Rev. Sociol. 27:363–85, 2001

Major B., O'Brien L.T., *The social psychology of stigma*, Department of Psychology, University of California, Santa Barbara, 2005

Masoli M., Fabian D., Holt S., Beasley R., *Global Burden of Asthma,* Medical Research Institute of New Zealand, University of Southampton (2004)

Pahl G. and Beitz W., *Engineering design: a systematic approach,* Springer, London, New York,1996.

Pope C.A., Burnett R.T., Thun M.J., Calle E.E., Krewski D., Ito K.,

Thurston G.D., *Lung cancer, cardiopulmonary mortality and long-term exposure to fine particulate air pollution*, Journal of the American Medical Association, 287(2002), 1132-1141

Pryor J.B., Reeder G. D., Yeadon C., Hesson-McInnis M, *A Dual-Process Model of Reactions to Perceived Stigma*, Illinois State University, 2004

Roozenburg N.F.M. and Eekels J., *Product design: fundamentals and methods.* Wiley, Chichester, New York, 1995

Schwartz J., Ballester F., Saez M., Pérez-Hoyos S., Bellido J., Cambra K., Arribas F., Canada A., Pérez-Boilos M.J., Sunyer J., *The concentration-response relation between air pollution and daily deaths.- Environmental Health Perspectives*, 109(2001), 1001-1005

Von Klot S. Wölke G., Tuch T., Heinrich J., Dockery D.W., Schwartz J., Kreylling W.G., Wichman H.E., Peters A.,- *Increased asthma medication use in association with ambient fine and ultrafine particles.-*, European Respiratory Journal, 20(2002), 691-702

Ward D.J., Ayres J.G., *Particulate air pollution and panel studies in children: a systematic review*, Occupational and Environmental Medicine 61:13, 2004

Wickman M., Lilja G., *Today, one child in four has an ongoing allergic disease in Europe. What will the situation be tomorrow?*, Allergy, 58(2003), 570-57

THE EFFECT OF THERMAL INERTIA ON ENERGY DEMAND AND THERMAL COMFORT IN DWELLINGS

Stijn Verbeke
University of Antwerp
Artesis University College of Antwerp
stijn.verbeke@artesis.be
–

Thermal mass of building constructions has the ability to store and release heat, depending on temperature difference with the surroundings. This doctoral research will assess the impact of thermal mass on yearly energy demand and thermal comfort in Belgian residential housing. Whole building simulation software EnergyPlus is used to model different geometries, constructions and occupant behaviour scenarios. The virtual experiment will result in guidelines on the desired level of thermal inertia and ways to achieve this.

KEYWORDS

Thermal inertia, Building simulation, EnergyPlus, comfort, Building Performance

INTRODUCTION

In 1998 the SENVIVV study revealed the dramatic state of thermal insulation in new Belgian residential building.[1] One decade later the attention for thermal insulation has risen sharply, due to the high cost of winter heating, growing environmental concern and legal requirements. The latter have become more stringent and were adapted to the European Energy Performance of Buildings Directive.

The traditional cavity wall building method is less suited as insulation thickness increases. As a promising alternative building method for low energy dwellings, light weight structures and especially wood frame building is swiftly gaining popularity in Belgian house building. As there is little experience with this building method in Belgium, debate is still going on regarding the benefits and drawbacks.

The low level of thermal mass compared to traditional building is often referred to as an important disadvantage. It is argued that a high thermal mass improves thermal comfort and reduces energy demand of buildings. Although certainly valid for office buildings, this statement requires closer investigation in regard to residential housing. One has to be very careful when interpreting research results concerning building thermal mass because conclusions may differ greatly depending on period of analysis, weather climate data used and occupant behaviour due to complex dynamic interactions. For example, a Swedish study concludes that a heavy weight house uses 20% less heating energy compared to a lightweight alternative while maintaining the same comfort level.[2] Conversely, Finney states high thermal mass will augment the heating energy demand of UK buildings by at least 10%.[3]

This research will investigate the impact of building thermal inertia in residential building over a whole year. Both occupants' thermal comfort and energy demand for space heating will be predicted for various configurations of geometries, construction composition and occupant behaviour.

CONTENT AND SUBJECT

The materials inside the building can absorb heat or release heat depending on the temperature difference with their surroundings. The amount of heat stored depends on the density [kg.m-3] and specific heat capacity [J.kg-1.K-1] of the material. The rate of heat exchange is influenced by the thermal conductivity [W.m-1.K-1] of the material. The thermal mass of a building can have large dynamic effects on the indoor climate of a building. The ability to time-shift temperature peaks is referred to as the *thermal inertia* of a building.

Thermal inertia of a building can be exploited to reduce the energy demand and improve thermal comfort of occupants. Especially in office buildings, characterised by a high internal heat load from people and electronic equipment, heat or cold storage have proven to be beneficial. New office buildings often include concepts such as night ventilation or concrete core activation. Night ventilation involves the circulation of fresh outside air at night to cool down the building structure in which heat is accumulated. This passive cooling method can prevent overheating without the need for an expensive active cooling system. Concrete core activation uses the thermal mass of concrete floors to allow for the use of embedded highly efficient low temperature heating systems and moderate temperature cooling systems. Even without these concepts, thermal inertia can provide better thermal comfort for the occupants because temperature peaks are flattened out and delayed in time.

Many argue that a high thermal mass is also beneficial to improve thermal comfort in a residential building. Thermal mass can indeed act as a thermal flywheel which dampens temperature fluctuations.

But compared to office buildings, internal thermal load in houses is fairly small and the amount of glazing is limited. Therefore, the overheating risk for Belgian houses is reduced to a small portion of the year, and can be further reduced by applying well designed sun shading. As this eliminates the need for an active cooling system, one cannot expect huge energy savings by incorporating thermal mass in the house. Furthermore, the occupancy of a house is very unpredictable compared to offices. People may be away at work, taking a shower, sleeping, etc. Instead of keeping a constant comfort temperature, fluctuating temperatures and intermittent heating can save fossil energy. So a building with low thermal inertia might as well provide better thermal comfort because

of the quicker reaction.

The effect of thermal inertia is not revealed by a steady state analysis, which solely assesses the thermal transmittance (U-value) of the external building surfaces. Assessing the dynamic behaviour of heat conduction, storage and release, requires solving the differential algebraic equations for time dependent heat transport.[4] Time dependency is caused by ever changing boundary conditions of external temperature, solar irradiation and internal heat load. In literature many attempts of analytically or semi-numerically solving these equations for simplified conditions are described.[5] The rapid progress of computer power made these methods obsolete. Several software codes are now capable of simulating solar irradiation, heat transport, heat storage and HVAC systems for whole buildings.

For this research a great flexibility is needed for programming own assumptions regarding user behaviour, in addition to a reliable calculation of heat storage and release at small time steps. After careful consideration whole-building energy simulation program EnergyPlus was chosen.[6] This software tool is developed by Lawrence Berkeley National Laboratory and others, funded by U.S. Department of Energy. For this research the simulation engine of EnergyPlus is used without any commercially available graphical user interface to retain maximum flexibility. Input files are manually composed with the freeware IDF editor.

The simulation kernel of EnergyPlus is validated according to BESTEST standards, but nevertheless the quality of the generated simulation results depends totally on the quality of the user input.[7] Therefore much research effort is directed to the assessment of impact and uncertainty of the input variables. A simplified model consisting of one room is constructed for this purpose.

Key variables include:

1. **Climate data**

   The simulation is carried out for a one year period. The weather data result from the Ashrae International Weather Year for Energy Calculations data for Brussels.

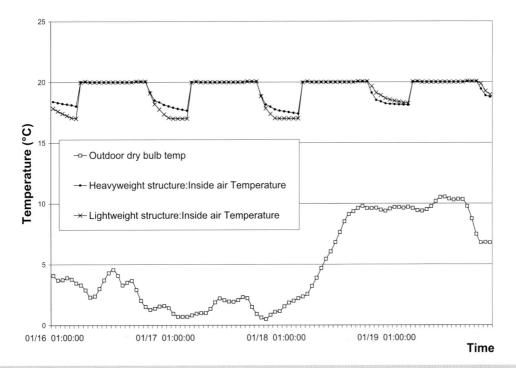

2. Building characterisation

Thermal behaviour of the building skin is governed by geometry of the building skin, window sizing and orientation and properties of building materials. As this research focuses on thermal inertia, estimated thermal mass of interior is also modelled. The heating system is simplified to a perfect heat production system, neglecting inertia of the water.

3. Occupant modelling

This research pays particular attention to the modelling of occupant behaviour. Stochastic models will be generated, e.g. resembling a couple working during office hours, or an elderly couple staying at home most of the time. Presence of the occupants in different rooms is scheduled. Related to this, the internal generated thermal load due to metabolism, lighting and appliances is modelled. Finally, interaction of occupants with heating and ventilation control systems will be programmed.

4. Simulation parameters

EnergyPlus needs some parameters to perform the simulations. A small time step of 5 minutes is chosen. The heating and ventilation systems are auto-sized based on winter and summer design day conditions. Further simulations will support the choice between conduction transfer functions and conduction finite differences as heat balance algorithm.

RESULTS AND DISCUSSION

Preliminary results show the different behaviour of a heavy weight and lightweight room. The graph shows a four day period during the heating season. The heat delivery system is simplified to a perfect convective system. Note the slower cool down reaction of the heavy weight building when the temperature set point is lowered intermittently.

The difference in yearly heating demand is less than 2%. This is expected to change as the model becomes more sophisticated, incorporating detailed user behaviour and a more realistic heating system. A model to assess year-round thermal comfort of inhabitants remains to be chosen.

So far the model consists of a single room. This will be expanded to a set of geometries corresponding with common houses and flats. Internal walls will be considered adiabatic, and a nodal airflow network will represent the convective heat exchanges between the different rooms.

CONCLUSION

Many people state thermal inertia is always beneficial, but it was argued this statement needs closer investigation in regard to residential building in the Belgian climate. Whole-building simulation tool EnergyPlus is used to predict human thermal comfort and energy use for different scenarios of house geometry, building materials and occupants.

If the effect of thermal inertia proves to be beneficial, research will focus on how the desired level of thermal inertia can be reached, even in light weight buildings. Different design options include: heavy weight internal walls, heavy weight floors, external wall claddings, phase change materials which are able to store and release latent heat, and partially underground building.[8] Finally, a cost/benefit analysis will be performed to select the most economic design strategy. ■

Ph.D Thesis Directors
Prof. dr. Aviel Verbruggen
UA-Faculty of Applied Economics Assoc.
Assoc. Prof. Ir.arch. Lucien Denissen
Artesis University College Antwerp

ACKNOWLEDGEMENTS

The author wishes to express his thanks to prof. dr. Aviel Verbruggen and ir.-arch. Lucien Denissen for their guidance. The financial support provided by the University of Antwerp RIOFI fund is also gratefully acknowledged.
references

ENDNOTES

1   WTCB, *Senvivv: Study of the Energy Aspects of New Dwellings in Flanders - Final Report*, Brussels, 1998

2   A. Norén, J. Akander, E. Isfält, and O. Söderström, *The Effect of Thermal Inertia on Energy Requirement in a Swedish Building - Results Obtained with Three Calculation Models*, International Journal of Low Energy and Sustainable Buildings, 1, 1999

3   P. Tuohy, L. McElroy and C. Johnstone, Thermal Mass, Insulation and Ventilation in Sustainable Housing - an Investigation across Climate and Occupancy 2005, 9th IBPSA conference, Montreal, 2005, pp.1253-1260

4   J. A Clarke, *Energy Simulation in Building Design*, Oxford, 2004

5   G. Guglielmini, U. Magrini, and E. Nannei, *The Influence of the Thermal Inertia of Building Structures on Comfort and Energy Consumption*, Journal of building physics, 5(2), 1981, pp.59-72.

6   D.B. Crawley, J. W. Hand., M. Kummert and B.T. Griffith, *Contrasting the Capabilities of Building Energy Performance Simulation Programs*, 9th IBPSA conference, Montreal, 2005

7   A.M. Malkawi and G. Augenbroe (eds.), *Advanced Building Simulation*, Oxfordshire, 2004

8   F. Kuznik, J. Virgone and J.-J. Roux, *Energetic Efficiency of Room Wall Containing Pcm Wallboard: A Full-Scale Experimental Investigation*, Energy and Buildings, 40(2), 2008, pp.148-156

ASSESSING DAYLIGHT AND FIRE SAFETY IN THE INTEGRATED ARCHITECTURAL DESIGN PROCESS OF ATRIA

Saskia Gabriël
Artesis University College of Antwerp
saskia.gabriel@artesis.be
–

Glass-covered spaces are frequently used in impressive building designs. However, the energy savings and also the fire safety of these buildings remain points of friction within the design process. Many studies have shown that large energy savings of buildings with atria can be realised by daylight optimisation and the use of the thermal buffer effect of atria.

Hence, the related design variables of daylighting and fire safety in atria are investigated with several methods. These will, in addition to a survey of the building industry, reveal the barriers, the advantages and the disadvantages of the currently used methods. An optimised system could possibly be discovered for daylight and fire safety.

Furthermore, results of experiments on daylight optimisation and design exercises of atrium buildings will lead to an integrated design methodology for architects in the early stages of the design, where decisions have the largest impact on the building's future energy use.

The aim of this research is to demonstrate the efficiency of such a methodology in the design of atrium buildings or glass-covered spaces for optimising daylighting and fire safety.

KEYWORDS
Atrium, Daylighting, Integrated design, Safety, Simulation.

INTRODUCTION

The most compelling reason for architects to insert an atrium in a building is to maximise daylight entry in adjacent spaces in order to reduce electrical lighting and cooling. Therefore, a study of the annual Daylight Factor (DF) in these spaces appears to be crucial to predict interior daylighting and thus the comfort of the future user.[1] The related design variables ought to be considered too; e.g. visual comfort, shading devices, furniture, weather conditions, surrounding buildings, verdure, etc.

Moreover, the complexity of atrium buildings finds its origin in the European legislation on the fire safety of atria. At present atrium buildings in Belgium can only be permitted on the basis of a deviation application. Thorough analyses are demanded, which indicates the importance of fire safety studies. Furthermore, it implies an active interest in the possibilities and barriers in performing hot smokeanalyses as part of an integrated design process.

This investigation also addresses the question of how a daylight optimisation system (e.g. light shelf, anidolic ceiling) can be designed for the atrium, without obstructing smoke evacuation.

The final aim of this doctoral research is the development of an efficient integrated design methodology for optimal daylight use and fire safety. This methodology will be applied to an atrium design. It could support the decisions in the early design process, which will be increasingly focused on sustainable building and energy management of buildings. One might assume that avoiding important decisions on daylighting and fire safety could reduce failure costs, energy use and construction time. In brief, introducing an atrium can potentially save energy and money, but requires thorough analyses - especially on daylight and fire safety - in the early design phases.[2]

CONTENT AND SUBJECT

Before starting the first experiments, a profound literature study was performed to assess the research topic.

The literature study also showed the importance of an Integrated Design and Building Process (IDBP) for complex buildings. This process can be assisted by Building Information Modelling (BIM) and specific forms of collaboration. In summary, we can assign several effects to the application of the IDBP. First of all, there are less failure costs in the building process because designers can better anticipate conflicts and construction problems. Second, there is improved communication and collaboration between the multi-disciplinary building teams due to the facilitated access to project information in different formats, and as a result, a lower threshold between the process stages. Lastly, maintenance problems can be solved during the design and will lead to an extended lifespan of the building.[3,4] While the enthusiasm for an IDBP continues to grow, there are also some disadvantages. First, the design process takes more time because of the analyses and the detail of the design. It could be argued that this is offset by the insight gained by the building owner and architect in the building. Also, the architect and the client receive increasing responsibilities and coordinating tasks in all the phases of the process.[5] We can conclude from this, that the IDBP has already found its way into the practice, but still needs some refinement and specification of tasks for complex projects.

Many research workers have indicated that daylight is the key factor to reduce internal heat gains and save energy in commercial buildings.[7] For atria, this can be particularly true when integrated into a renovation programme. However, the design of atria for energy saving purposes requires a great

FIGURE 1: THE TECHNICAL UNIVERSITY OF TRONDHEIM, ELA-BUILDING[6]

deal of attention and knowledge from the architect and the building team.

Researchers have also looked at the aspects of smoke and heat extraction in atrium buildings. Since safety should be addressed as a primary design factor for atria, know-how and insight in the process of combustion of atrium-fires is essential.[8]

This study suggested that further research on the combination of daylighting and fire safety in an atrium design is required. Often, these two aspects are given a different approach in the early stages of the design and are found difficult to combine. It appeared interesting to investigate how these should be treated in the IDBPphases and how they can be optimised while taking into account all the variables.

As a first research step, the investigation of daylight in atrium buildings was undertaken. To start experimenting with the chosen software (Ecotect with export to the validated Radiance program), the most frequent atrium typologies were identified, which are shown in Fig. 2.

From this, conceptual BIMs are designed. These are currently being assessed for their exportation capabilities. They will later be investigated for daylight variables, and optimised for daylighting.

Secondly, the possible daylight systems will be looked at. It will be assessed how an innovative daylight system can be designed and applied, without obstructing smoke evacuation in the atrium. The aim is to find an innovative daylight system for a linear atrium typology.

Then, using zone-models and field-models, the atrium typologies will be reviewed. These models are designed to gain an insight into smoke and heat dispersion in case of fire. This study will show that several design measures implemented earlier for daylight will have to be adjusted in order to ensure fire safety. An atrium building can only be permitted on the basis of a deviation application, unless a Smoke and Heat Extraction Ventilation System (SHEVS) and and a sprinkler system are installed in the atrium. Since both installations have counteracting effects, it is important to develop a system that integrate the necessary fire safety analyses in the early stages of the design.

Finally, solutions to the barriers and maximised use of the advantages of the methods, which are now used in practice, will be translated into a methodology for optimisation of daylight and fire safety in atrium design. This will be useful for the architect to keep up with growing liabilities and tasks in the design of complex buildings.

Lastly, the elaborated methodology will be applied to a new atrium building design to show that it is practicable. It will concern a complex atrium typology with daylight optimisation systems and SHEVS in combination with natural ventilation. The annual heating and cooling load will be minimised by any means. If necessary, passive heating and cooling will be applied.

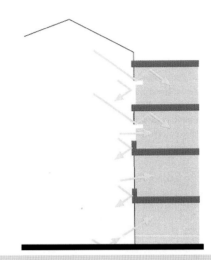

FIGURE 3: LIGHT REFLECTION ON LIGHT SHELVES IN AN ATRIUM

RESULTS AND DISCUSSION

The first results of the export of BIMs to Ecotect/Radiance were disappointing. Due to the huge enthusiasm of the building industry, many software developers have integrated the export possibilities. But there still exist so many barriers and disadvantages that use of this export function is not yet profitable. This will, however, change very soon, and it is therefore important for architects to keep up with the rapidly evolving software.

From the preliminary daylight studies, it was observed that the shape and geometry of the atrium was of great influence on daylight penetration in the adjacent spaces of the atrium. This implies that decisions on daylight should be made early on in the design process. The same conclusion is expected for fire safety.[9]

Thus, facilitated use of BIM in the IDBP is a step forward in designing complex atrium buildings, where optimised daylight can help save energy and assessed fire safety can help save lives and reduce maintenance costs.

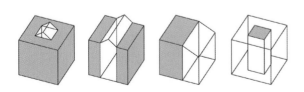

FIGURE 2: MOST FREQUENTLY USED SIMPLIFIED TYPOLOGIES

CONCLUSION

By developing a methodology for an optimised Integrated Design and Building Process, a complex atrium with optimum features can be designed. By assessing daylight and fire safety, one could come to a well-considered atrium building and gain insight into the problems that arise when combining the variables.

By applying the knowledge acquired with the use of the methodology in the design process, an architect can gain fame and experience for future energy-saving projects. ∎

Ph.D Thesis Directors
Prof. Dr. Aviel Verbruggen
UA-Faculty of Applied Economics
Assoc. Prof. ir. arch. Lucien Denissen
Artesis University College of Antwerp

REFERENCES

1. Ander GD., *Daylighting performance and design*, New York: Van Nostrand Reinhold; 1995. 241 p.

2. Baker N., Steemers K., *Energy and Environment - A technical Design Guide,* London: E & FN Spon; 2000. 224 p.

3. Howell I., Batcheler B., *Building Information Modeling Two Years Later. Huge Potential, Some Success and Several Limitations*, University of Utah; 2005. p 1-9.

4. Scheer DR., *Building Information Modeling: What About Architecture?*, 2005. p 3-6.

5. Bash K., *Architecture as a second language - enabling integrated design*, In: DMS Architects i, ed., 2007.

6. Blesgraaf P., *Grote Glasoverkapte Ruimten (GGR)*, Sittard: Nederlandse Onderneming Voor Energie en Milieu bv (NOVEM), 1996, 125 p.

7. Samant S., Yang F., *Daylighting in atria: The effect of atrium geometry and reflectance distribution*, in: Lighting Research and Technology 2007;39(2): pp.147-157.

8. Saxon R., *Atrium buildings: Development and design,* London, The Architectural Press, 1986, 198 p.

9. Dubocentrum, *Integraal ontwerpen: proces tot een duurzaam gebouwde omgeving*, 2007.

OPTIMISING SUSTAINABILITY IN GROUP HOUSING

ADS
19/20

Bart Janssens
Artesis University College of Antwerp
bart.janssens@artesis.be
–

The study of translating and optimising sustainability in group housing projects begins with the development and definition of components and their indicators for sustainable construction in group housing. On the basis of this broadening of the umbrella concepts of sustainability and group housing, design guidelines for future projects will be developed after case studies have been executed. This will be followed by design scientific research in which certain aspects of sustainability are examined in greater depth. These could relate to cultural, sociological, constructional, building physical, ecological, economic and/or policy aspects.

KEYWORDS

Architecture, group housing, durability, optimisation, design scientific research

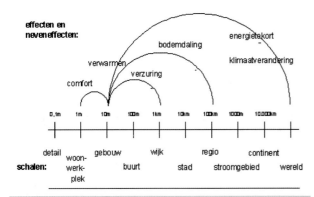

ILLUSTRATION 1: ENERGY EFFECTS AND SIDE EFFECTS IN ALL THE SCALES

INTRODUCTION

Global warming has far-reaching implications for our environment. To avoid mortgaging the well-being of future generations the United Nations has placed sustainable development high on the agenda. Within the field of architecture too there is a growing realisation that sustainability should be an important aspect of our housing culture.

In other words, the environment problem has become a compelling starting point for the design, realisation and maintenance of buildings. In the development of sustainable architecture today an important sector is often omitted: building projects for group housing, both private and public. The role played by grouped housing is gradually dominating the housing sector. It is therefore of great importance that this sector commits itself to sustainable building.

The aim of this doctoral study therefore is focused on one of the most important and most challenging architectonic problems: how can sustainable architecture be translated into attached housing projects? How can sustainability be optimised in group housing?

CONTENT AND SUBJECT

The study of translating sustainability into group housing will generally be divided into two parts, with part one laying the foundation for the actual design scientific research.

This basis will on the one hand be formed by a clear definition of a number of related concepts. By way of a purposive study of literature it will develop a clear terminology associated with the umbrella concepts of group housing and sustainability. Here the main point will be the development and defining of components for sustainable building in group housing. Indicators for each of these components will then be examined, reproduced and defined. This theoretical approach will also be tested and corroborated by way of practical examples.

On the other hand, purposive case studies associated with sustainable group housing will be used to provide a clear picture of sample projects that have already been completed or are still in the process of being built. This will be supplemented with surveys and interviews with housing companies, promoters and residents in order to achieve project sheets that will give us clear insight into the problems related to the sustainability of housing projects. An important part of this study will be spent on determining and verifying the marginal criteria predetermined by the actors themselves on the one hand, and on the other hand, the broadened components regarding sustainability.

The bottlenecks within the broadening of the concept of sustainability in group housing that are brought to light through evaluation will then be examined more closely with the aim of developing possible solutions. The result of this optimisation is an immediate applicability in the cases dealt with as well as helping to form a basis for the development of design guidelines.

A study of optimisation will also initiate further design scientific research based on the conclusions regarding sustainability in group housing projects.

In part two the immediate problem-solving study will be followed by a greater in-depth study of specific aspects of sustainability within a predetermined form of group housing. A design scientific research method will be used in this further specialisation. Once it has been made more concrete the results will be tested by way of an evaluation study.

RESULTS AND DISCUSSION

The results in view are to be found in three domains:

First and foremost a clear and recognisable analysis and a broadening of general existing and acceptable basic building blocks (*People, Planet, Prosperity, Participation, Project*) need to be defined within the umbrella concept of sustainable development, thereby producing a clear, manageable and inspiring instrumentation for the realisation of aspects of

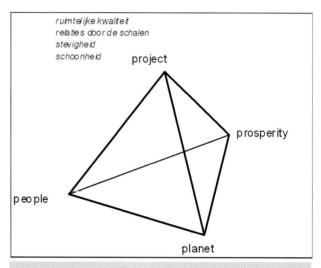

ILLUSTRATION 2: SUSTAINABLE BUILDING SINCE OSLO 2002

sustainability in group housing. A second result will be formed mainly through optimising the cases and sample projects dealt with. On the basis of this and the formerly developed theoretical instrumentation, practically-oriented design guidelines (design-related and constructional) for future sustainable group housing projects will be developed.

The choice for further design scientific research specialisation depends on the one hand on the study of, and on the other hand the results of, the design guidelines: one or more critical bottlenecks, a holistic approach that is possible or not, a necessary evolution, and so on. Possible fields of study are:

- Social sustainability in housing projects with high densities: The recently developed policy visions are increasingly based on greater densities within building projects. However on the scale of the building this starting point should be subject to in-depth examination especially with regard to quality of life, social interaction, green areas, multi-culturalism, and so on. Specific design guidelines for social sustainability will be developed by way of an applicable case in stacked housing.

- Sustainability in stacked housing projects: As a result of the memorandum on high-rise blocks which is still being drafted for the city of Antwerp and the growing interest in the specific typology of high-rise buildings, it is essential that we examine how sustainability can acquire form within these projects. Based on a holistic approach to the concept of sustainability, the formerly drafted instrumentation, case studies that have been executed and those which by necessity have yet to be executed, a total design will be developed from which specific design guidelines can be synthesised for sustainable stacked housing.

- Social sustainability in housing projects with a high density: applicable case: high-rise buildings
- Sustainability in function of the urban development context of a building
- Development of a design methodology for the integration of passive and active measures for energy control in group housing in an urban context. ■

Ph.D Thesis Directors
Prof. dr. Aviel Verbruggen
UA-Faculty of Applied Economics
Assoc. Prof. ir.arch. Lucien Denissen
Artesis University College of Antwerp

REFERENCES

Achterberg W., 'Samenleving, Natuur en Duurzaamheid', z.p.

Arda J., Fernandez Per A., Mozas J., 'Dbook, Density Data Diagrams Dwelling', z.p., 2007

Busby P., Taggart J., 'Learning Sustainable Design', z.p., 2007

Gonzalo R., Haberman K.J., 'Architecture énergétiquement efficient: Bases pout la conception en la construction', z.p., 2007

Moughtin J.C., 'Urban Design', z.p., 2004

Neelen M, Van Hinte E., Vink J., Vollaard P., 'Smart Architecture', z.p., 2003,

Ponting C., Van De Weijer R., 'A Green History of the World', z.p., 1994

Rossi, A., 'L'architettura della città', Padua, 1966

Soderstrom M., 'Green City', z.p., 2006

Steiner F., 'Human Ecology', z.p., 2002

DESIGN METHODOLOGY IN THE DIGITAL ARCHITECTURAL PRACTICE

Kathleen De Bodt
Artesis University College of Antwerp
kathleen.debodt@artesis.be
—

The subject of this Ph.D. addresses the way in which digital techniques and methodologies can be integrated into the conceptual stage of the architectural design process. Accordingly, research is conducted into digital design procedures and techniques, the correlation between theory and practice in the field of digital architectural design, and the influence of digital design theory and processes on the complexity and spatial variation of design solutions. The research methods used in this thesis include literature studies, case studies, software and design process analyses, and are intended to answer the prevailing questions raised by the general preference and application of complex curved geometry in digital design projects.

KEYWORDS
CAAD, Digital Design, Design Methodology, Conceptual Design, Design Processes

INTRODUCTION
Since the introduction of the personal computer, interactive and digital media have become instrumental in the investigation of architectural design decisions and solutions. Numerous techniques have been introduced in CAAD and related software, allowing different ways for generating, testing, comparing, validating and challenging design solutions through the use of computer visualisation, simulation, analysis and evaluation. These newly emerging possibilities have raised important questions regarding design, and as Oxman (2006) argues, there is a need to consider a new understanding of the nature of design when using digital media. Consequently, it has become imperative to study the application and implementation of these techniques and processes. Therefore, the thesis aims to develop an insight and increase the understanding of the concepts and ideas that are fundamental to digital architectural design, focusing in particular on the innovative use of advanced software functionality in designs that were created in the 1990 to 2000 decade. Likewise, the study tries to answer the prevailing questions raised by the predominant presence of complex curved geometry and attempts to trace why and in what way digital techniques and concepts have stimulated an overall preference for this particular kind of formal expression. Also, because the preliminary findings of the study showed a general disregard of the use of sound and acoustics in digital design, an inquiry is made into how these can be instrumental when implemented in a digital design process.

The added value of the research activity to the general knowledge in the field of conceptual architectural design will include a better understanding of the way in which current architectural theory and design methodology relate to digital design. The findings will also contribute to the digital professionalism of the architectural design practice by increasing the know-how of the possibilities and applications of advanced modelling, visualisation and generative computation techniques. Also, several software applications are created as an addition to existing CAAD software.

CONTENT AND SUBJECT

First of all, an outline of the digital design research field was made based on an extensive literature study of both primary and secondary sources regarding digital architects and digital design from 1990 to 2000. The number of publications on the subject of digital design is extensive. They describe and comprehensively illustrate digital design projects, but scientific publications on digital design methodology and processes are lacking. The way in which digital techniques and process were applied is merely mentioned, without sufficiently explaining the methodology and software techniques, making it altogether impossible to analyse, understand or recreate the design process. In addition, a full survey and classification of the large number of digital design approaches, each in themselves supported by different digital techniques and software functionality, is missing.

As Jones (1992) points out, many of the new methods in design are taken from other disciplines. Likewise, digital design concepts were considered in the context of contemporary science, philosophy, cultural and social changes, and architectural theory, in particular regarding the position which digital design takes with reference to critical and non-critical, projective architecture.

From the literature study a selection of digital architectural practices was made based on the design processes and techniques that were presented. Next, a number of designs were selected according to the particular process that was implemented. The design outcome was studied along with the prevailing design concepts and elaboration of the projects in order to ascertain the main concepts of the designers. These concepts were then further analysed and evaluated with reference to key theoretical architectural notions and texts.

In order to explore the new ways of architectural expression, form finding and communication integrated in the design processes, several digital design techniques were analysed and reconstructed. The functionality of the tools which the designers used was analysed to ascertain the principles, techniques and methodology of the digital design processes that were set up. These processes were then recreated using various software including 3dsMax and Blender 3D.

Digitally designed projects presented in publications all seem to look alike. Most of them freely use complex curved geometry, the application of which can only partially be explained by the availability of NURBS tools in recent software. Furthermore, the publications indicate that all kinds of information are being used to generate designs, but examples of processes driven by acoustic data or sound analysis are rare. At the same time, the analysis of CAAD and advanced visualisation and modelling software show almost a total lack of audio related tools. This demonstrated the need to study the requirements and possible ways of implementing these issues. This was done through case studies in a number of project related classes at the TU Delft, in workshops conducted during consecutive ADSL workshop weeks at the Higher Institute of Architectural Sciences Henry van de Velde, and within the frame of Digital Design Master classes.

The study of audio and acoustics in CAAD and digital design relies on the analysis of acoustic software and the literature study of papers and dissertations on the subject of 3D audio

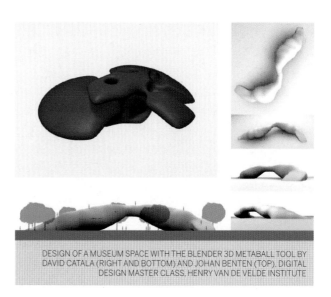

DESIGN OF A MUSEUM SPACE WITH THE BLENDER 3D METABALL TOOL BY DAVID CATALA (RIGHT AND BOTTOM) AND JOHAN BENTEN (TOP). DIGITAL DESIGN MASTER CLASS, HENRY VAN DE VELDE INSTITUTE

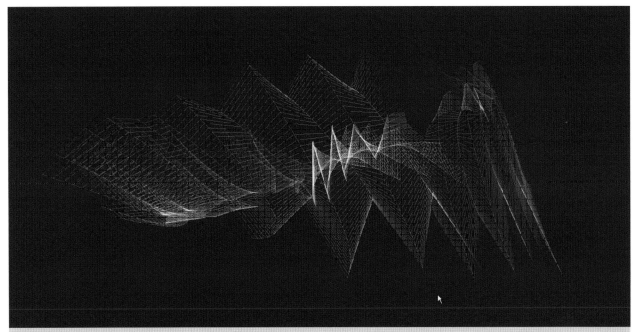

3D PROTOTYPE OF A NURB SURFACE DEFORMED BY SOUND PARAMETERS, CREATED USING THE PLAN-B APPLICATION WHICH WAS DEVELOPED IN MAX/MSP.
PRESENTED AT THE ASCAAD 2007 CONFERENCE IN ALEXANDRIA, EGYPT

computation, auralisation and visualisation of sound in virtual environments and simulations. The possibilities of existing software such as game-engines, scripting and graphical programming environments were analysed and evaluated by developing and testing several applications.

RESULTS AND DISCUSSION

Several papers have been published and presented at international conferences and journals. A number of workshops on the subject of digital design were held, which allowed the assessment and testing of both existing and newly developed software, such as the SoundMatrix tool, which was created in the Max/MSP and Jitter graphical programming environment and tested in the InteAction workshop.

CONCLUSION

Work on the analysis and definition of specifications for a 3D sound application is still in progress. At the same time, a full draft is being compiled, assembling all previously collected information together with the published and unpublished written material. This process brings to light all necessary additions, changes and editing, which are being executed. ■

Ph.D Thesis Directors
Prof. ir. Leen van Duin (TU Delft)
Prof.ir.arch. msc Richard Foqué
Artesis University College of Antwerp
Prof. Dr. ir. arch. Piet Lombaerde
Artesis University College of Antwerp

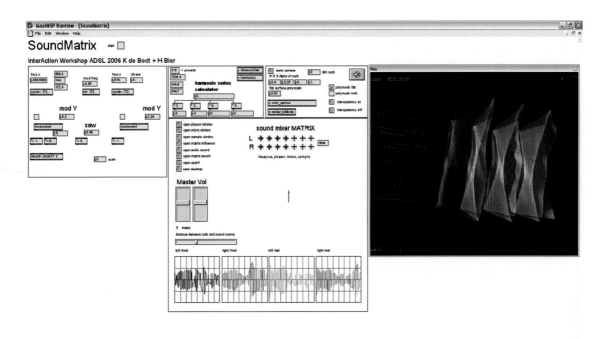

REFERENCES

H. Bier, K. De Bodt en J. Galle, 'Space Customizer, InterActive', in: A. Ali en C.A. Brebbia (eds), *Digital Architecture and Construction*, Southampton, 2006, pp.21-28

H. Bier, K. De Bodt en J. Galle, 'Prototypes for interactive architecture", in: H. Zha et al. (eds.) *Interactive Techologies and Sociotechnical Systems*, Xi'an, 2006, pp.21-28.

J.C. Jones, *Design Methods*, New York, 1992, p. xix.

K. De Bodt, 'Urban Sound[e]scape', in: F. Claessens en L. van Duin (eds.), *The European City, Architectural Interventions and transformations*, Delft, 2004, pp. 308-311.

K. De Bodt, 'Digital Resonance: Sound Parameters in Architectural Design', in: K. Oosterhuis en L. Feireiss (eds.), *Game Set and Match II*, Rotterdam, 2006, pp. 226-233.

K. De Bodt, 'Soundscapes and Architectural Spaces', in: V. Bourdakis en D. Charitos (eds.), *Communicating Spaces*, Volos, 2006, pp. 684-689

K. De Bodt en S. Lee, 'Plan_B: The Architectonic display of sonic information', in: A. Okeil, A. Aghlab Al-Attili en Z. Mallasi (eds.), *Em'body'ing Virtual Architecture*, Alexandrië, 2007, pp. 587-594.

K. De Bodt, 'Everything Flows: the influence of digital concepts and techniques on architectural education, research and design methodology', in: ICAE 2007 conference proceedings, Beijing, 2007

R. Oxman, 'Educating the Digital Design Thinker, What Do We Teach When We Teach Design', in: V. Bourdakis en D. Charitos (eds), *Communicating Spaces*, Volos, 2006, pp. 198-205.

ADS
19/20

ON THE DIALECTICS OF URBANICITY AND CREATIVE AGENCY, THEORIZING THEIR RELATIONSHIP & FORMULATING A METHODOLOGICAL APPROACH

Koenraad Keignaert
Artesis University College of Antwerp
koenraad.keignaert@artesis.be
–

The goal is to demonstrate through case studies that the respective patterns of economic growth of cities and their state of urban fitness with regard to their local economies result from (dis-)similarities in the socio-cultural embedded nature of habitual, creative and innovative practices.

But, dynamic and innovative human practices play an evermore important role in the creation of local wealth. Scientific findings suggest strong correlations between several, at first sight, unrelated phenomena; technology, talent and tolerance. We take these findings to be indicative of socio-cultural structures wherein practices of innovation are embedded. We are particularly interested in the role of the 'creative class' within the local economic and socio-cultural structures.

KEYWORDS

Complex adaptive systems, Emergence, Extelligence, Sustainability, Urban economics

INTRODUCTION

The goal is to demonstrate through case studies that the respective patterns of economic growth of cities and their state of urban fitness with regard to their local economies result from (dis-) similarities in the socio-cultural embedded nature of habitual, creative and innovative practices.

The growth path of a particular city's economy more often than not differs from that of other cities. Local natural endowments and other such objectively measurable features can partly explain the differences away. But, dynamic and innovative human practices play an evermore important role in the creation of local wealth. Findings by R. Florida, aiming to explain the growth paths of 50 US cities, suggest strong correlations between several, at first sight, unrelated phenomena; technology, talent and tolerance. We take these findings to be indicative of socio-cultural structures wherein practices of innovation are embedded. We are particularly interested in the role of the 'creative class' within the local economic and socio-cultural structures.

Cities are open systems, i.e. they are mutable under pressure from processes that take place both within its confines and outside its boundaries. Implementing urban economic policies –based on general economic findings– while neglecting a city's deeper socio-cultural structures could, due to the complexity and interdependent nature of economic urban competitiveness

ADS
19/20

and social coherence or equity, just as well dampen as stimulate the urban fitness, the local growth path, and the agential innovative practices. Historicity is important to this project and therefore an attempt will be made to anchor the studied socio-economic processes within the framework of the Kondratieff long waves.

To elucidate the social structures that generate the observed growth path and urban fitness; and searching to offer more explanatory depth, we have chosen to tackle this question intensively, i.e. through the study of a limited number of cases (Amsterdam & Antwerp).

CONTENT AND SUBJECT

The author lectures in fields of economics and sociology at the Department of Design Sciences of the University College of Antwerp. Right at the start of his tenure, the author felt challenged by the question how the eventual professional efforts of the Department's graduates related to and where influence by the urban setting wherein they worked and lived. A tentative – although its author intended it otherwise – response was formulated by Richard Florida. His answer seemingly offers city officials a formula to assure their city's economic prosperity. Some strong correlations between several, at first sight, unrelated phenomena – technology, talent and tolerance – inspired him to declare that we are witnesses to the dawn of the creative society. The *Creative Class* – whereof architects and product developers are most certainly members – is particularly demanding of 'over-all urban quality of life' when choosing a place to live and work. He suggests that a city is a social engineering problem, requiring some fine-tuning by enlightened spirits, which however, wholly disregards the city's path dependent nature. The aim is to offer a comprehensive framework to theorize on and to formulate a methodological approach to the dialectic relationship between urbanicity and creative agency. Thereby we wish to demonstrate that cities' respective patterns of economic growth and their state of urban fitness with regard to their local economies result from (dis-)similarities in the socio-cultural embedded nature of habitual, creative and innovative practices. Moreover, topics such as social equity, governance, sustainability and urban planning are part and parcel of the submitted research question.

However, any answer starts out by sketching the role and modi operandi of urban inhabitants. We start from extelligence, which is both the sum of all the forms of human capital - present and past - and the capability to presently or in the future add to it or change it. We define emergence as the phenomenon whereby a system apparently transcends anything that can be offered by its components. A city is a system wherefrom recombinations of meta-capitals (specifically relational, intelligence and identity capitals which are mostly of a tacit nature) and productive capitals (e.g. natural resources, finance, labour, and knowledge capital) emerge. We envisage these recombinations as either tangible (saleable) outcomes or intangible (untraded) interdependencies – i.e. potentially advantageous outcomes from tacit meta-capitals and face-to-face contacts. In his seminal work, Cities in Civilization, Sir P. Hall illustrates how certain cities through specific socio-cultural structures –mostly resulting from untraded interdependencies– were apt at reaping the benefits of an era.

This topic lies at the intersection of urban planning, economics and sociology. Each of these fields needs to be explored for its potential contributions. One major stumbling block has been the blatant divide that has grown in the second half of the 20th century between the social sciences on the one hand and on the other hand economics. The contributions are based on different ontologies, i.e. ways in which the functioning of human agents in social and economic settings is envisaged. This has led to seeing the city as a derelict remnant of capitalism at one extreme of the continuum and as an irrelevant entity at the other end; respectively in sociology and economics. Formulating a theoretical framework for this thesis is thus extremely challenging. However, in the outlying corners of both the social and economic scientific fields researchers have been turning to the field of biology and the techniques of simulation to find a new drive. Much has been written on Complex Adaptive Systems (CAS) in biology and simulation studies from the beginning of the 1980's, but it is only now that in both sociology and economics that the general ideas of CAS are being adopted. There is little doubt in the mind of the author that society at large is a prime example of CAS; and, so are cities. CAS is a promising approach for al the social sciences because it offers a way to integrate emergent phenomena, of which untraded interdependencies are an illustration.

Much of the current practice in urban planning is concerned with rejuvenation and renewal of urban neighborhoods. These projects are influence by the rapid evolution in the local and global economic textures through increased calls for creativity and innovation. Rightly so, the question is being asked how to relate spatial transformation to socio-cultural and economic innovation. Factually, we're dealing with a dialectic relationship here: innovative processes –whether private or public or both– drive the need for spatial transformation and spatial transformations enable or constrain potential processes. Spatial transformations resulting from innovation usually come at a cost: e.g. gentrification, loss of historical identity, increased competition over (abandonment of) spaces with desired (undesirable) attributes. Any public debate will inevitably revolve around the question whether spatial transformation or morphogenese –thus standing in contrast to morphostasis– is at all times the sole answer to innovative processes. Assuming that the implementation of socio-cultural and economic behavioural patterns is generally supported by spatial configurations, every spatial transformation requires a thorough understanding of the evolution of behavioural patterns –in particular of creative agency– and of historically inherited social structures which have resulted from prior creative agency. The author feels that the latter requisite has been completely or partially disregarded in all three scientific fields. Herein lays then the challenge: if we want to understand how members of the creative class influence the making of a city and vice versa we need to understand how human creativity in general creates a city and how a city constrains and enables its inhabitants in their functioning.

RESULTS AND DISCUSSION

In line with the theoretical difficulties it turns out that much of the available statistical data from the limited number of case studies is not adapted to analysis within a CAS-framework or is non-existent. It is impossible to remedy this even within the framework of a doctoral thesis. The remainder of the thesis – after the study of the existent literature and the formulation of a theoretical framework – is therefore of a qualitative rather than a quantitative nature. We hope to show that members of the creative class hold subjective ideas and views on the city where the work and that, at least in part, these ideas and views can explain their locational choices. The locational choices of creative agents in their turn influence the urban economic output. ∎

Ph.D Thesis Directors
Prof. dr. Luc Goossens
University of Antwerp
Prof. dr. ir. ar. Piet Lombaerde
Artesis University College of Antwerp

REFERENCES

Boddy M. & Parkinson M., *City matters. Competitiveness, cohesion and urban governance*, Bristol (UK), 2004.

Beinhocker E. D., *The origin of wealth. Evolution, complexity and the radical remaking of economics,* London (UK), 2007.

Carillo F. J., A Capital system for Monterrey. In Carrillo F. J. (editor) *Knowledge cities: Approaches, experiences and perspectives*, Burlington, Massachusetts (USA), 2006.

Florida R., *Cities and the creative class*, New York (USA), 2004.

Healey P., *Urban complexity and spatial strategies: Towards a relational planning for our times*, London (UK), 2007.

Kondratieff N., The long waves in economic life, in *Review of Economic Statistics*, Vol. 17, 1935, pp. 105-115.

O'Brien P. (ed.), *Urban Achievement in Early Modern Europe: Golden Ages in Antwerp, Amsterdam and London*, Cambridge (UK), 2001.

Sawyer R. K., *Social emergence: Societies as complex systems*, Cambridge (UK), 2005.

Schumpeter J., *Business cycles: A theoretical, historical and statistical analysis of the capitalist process*, New York (USA), 1939.

Stewart I. & Cohen J., *Figments of reality*, Cambridge (UK), 1997.

RESEARCH INTO THE USABILITY OF QUALITATIVE RESEARCH METHODS FROM SOCIOLOGY FOR ANALYSIS AND DESIGN WITHIN TOWN PLANNING

Katrijn Apostel
Artesis University College of Antwerp
katrijn.apostel@artesis.be
–

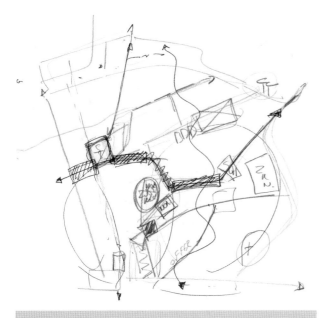

SKETCHES OF ANTWERP NORTH EAST FROM THE EXPERIENCE RESEARCH, DRAWN BY FOUR RESPONDENTS WHO KNOW THE AREA

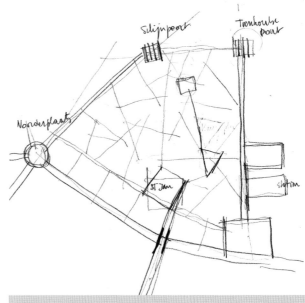

SKETCHES OF ANTWERP NORTH EAST FROM THE EXPERIENCE RESEARCH, DRAWN BY FOUR RESPONDENTS WHO KNOW THE AREA

This doctoral project will commence in November 2008 and will be conducted by Katrijn Apostel as a continuation of her master's thesis, entitled 'Experience research as a tool for analysis and design' as part of the Town and Area Planning course at the Hoger Instituut voor Architectuurwetenschappen, Henry van de Velde. This master's thesis examines the added value of experience research in the analysis of a well-defined space (in this case: Antwerp North East) and its design (structural outline).

This study will explore this topic in more depth in an interdisciplinary manner. Thus, the thesis will make an exhaustive study of existing qualitative methods and techniques from qualitative

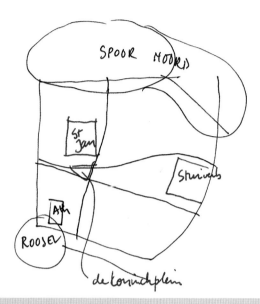

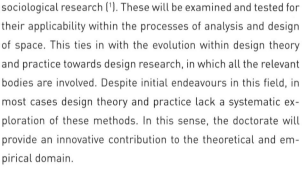

SKETCHES OF ANTWERP NORTH EAST FROM THE EXPERIENCE RESEARCH,
DRAWN BY FOUR RESPONDENTS WHO KNOW THE AREA

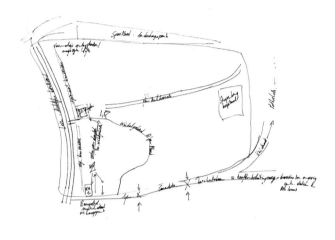

SKETCHES OF ANTWERP NORTH EAST FROM THE EXPERIENCE RESEARCH,
DRAWN BY FOUR RESPONDENTS WHO KNOW THE AREA

sociological research ([1]). These will be examined and tested for their applicability within the processes of analysis and design of space. This ties in with the evolution within design theory and practice towards design research, in which all the relevant bodies are involved. Despite initial endeavours in this field, in most cases design theory and practice lack a systematic exploration of these methods. In this sense, the doctorate will provide an innovative contribution to the theoretical and empirical domain.

By making use of the methods which have developed from sociology and environmental psychology, the thesis establishes a direct link between sociology, geography, architecture and town planning.

KEYWORDS

Qualitative research methods, Sociology, Analysis and design, Town planning

---

[1]   Research group Stad en Architectuur, *Catalogus van methoden en tech-nieken van het stadsonderzoek*, Leuven.

INTRODUCTION

Design means working through a process, the aim of which is to obtain a product. The context and the aim of the design process within town planning is space. The manner in which a town planning design is understood is therefore also directly linked to the manner in which the space is perceived.

The analysis of the space usually takes place from the top down, by taking an overall view, from which it can be abstracted. As an extension of this, town and area planners think in terms of bringing structure to the city so that it becomes a controllable collection of ordered components. By abstracting this from the complex city fabric, its specificity is not always recognised. Even though morpho-typological research, which primarily consists of drawing up the planning context, such as various morphology maps, intended purpose, etc., provides very useful information, which feeds the design, there is still a big void. In this way, analytical maps can indeed provide information on the functional importance of a building, but they are unable to convey the importance of the building for the users of that area. Would it therefore be possible to leave behind this abstract,

ADS
19/20

theoretical position of looking at a city? Would the bottom-up approach, from the aspect of everyday life, with its associated spontaneity, diversity and lack of order provide an alternative to this, or could it at least be complementary to it?[2] By gaining insight into the various groups and living habits that are present in the city, is a new dimension being added to the 'city space' concept[3]? Is it possible to map out the specific identities of various cities by analysing the city experience from the point of view of its users? After all, these are less clear to read in an abstract representation of the city space, which has the same characteristics in any city. Finally, is it easier to take these local identities into account at the design stage?

CONTENT

The actual knowledge concerning the usability of methods and techniques within experience research in the course of the analysis and design process of the space will be gained during the research into the specific problems and vice versa. This interaction translates into a twofold methodology, based upon two components: (Part 1) literature research into the qualitative methods and techniques which are applicable and (Part 2) designing research based on the operationalisation of the methods and techniques previously researched and selected.

The purpose of this designing research is to investigate whether it is possible to draw up a general method for the experience research and to what extent this qualitative research can (partly) replace the quantitative or whether it can at least be complementary to it. This is why the designing research also has to include morpho-typological research, so that the results from these two methods can be confronted and compared with each other.

Research into the substance of the subjective experience of a transformed spatial environment should be aimed more at the specificity and diversity of the areas. The focus of the research will also undoubtedly have to be diversified in accordance with

specific morphological characteristics of an environment and the scale of the design. [4] Generalising the research results is therefore also not necessary, given that it aims exactly at their indicative value in relation to the design or plan proposal. Use will be made of up-to-date computer techniques and associated software which will simplify the operationalisation and processing of the research results.

CASES

The applicability and the importance of the methods and techniques retained can only be demonstrated by applying these specifically to a number of cases. The main area of study will be Antwerp, given the wealth of knowledge that the Henry of the Velde-instituut holds on this city. This institute and the City of Antwerp also work together in partnership. The cases can therefore also be continued to be selected in liaison with the city, so that this study can also represent added value for them.

Cases can subsequently also be worked out in similar, medium-sized cities in order to thus achieve comparative research. The cities currently being considered are Amsterdam and Rotterdam. Two other smaller port towns have also been selected, i.e. Zeebrugge and Den Helder.

RESULTS AND POINTS FOR DISCUSSION

This project investigates what place qualitative sociological and social-psychological methods could take in comparison to the traditional methods of analysis, such as morpho-typological or historical research. The methods and techniques which have to be used for this purpose will be logged and operationalised on the basis of designing research involving the drawing up of structural sketches, city designs, 'landscape quality plans', etc.

The project is socially relevant because it investigates in which way the users of the space can be involved in area planning. ∎

2   T. Avermaete, 'Het zichtbare en het onzichtbare', *Oase*, 58, 2002, p. 5.
3   A. Madanipour, *Design of urban space: an inquiry into a socio-spatial process*, p. 73.

4   H. Van Geel, *Een sociaal cultureel uitstapje langs de gevels van nieuwe stedelijkheid*, Brussel.

ADS
19/20

Figures 1, 2, 3, 4:
Sketches of Antwerp North East from the experience research,
drawn by four respondents who know the area.
Figure 5:
Sought-after spatial structure for Antwerp North East as
a result of, for example, the sketches from the experience
research.

Ph.D Thesis Directors
Prof. Dr. An Verhetsel (UA)
Prof. Dr.ir.arch.Piet Lombaerde
Artesis University College Antwerp
UA

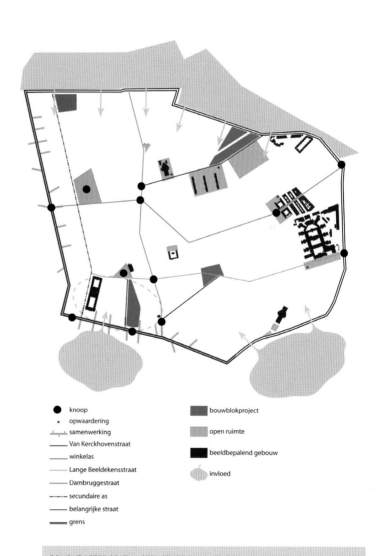

● knoop	bouwblokproject
★ opwaardering	open ruimte
samenwerking	beeldbepalend gebouw
Van Kerckhovenstraat	invloed
winkelas	
Lange Beeldekensstraat	
Dambruggestraat	
secundaire as	
belangrijke straat	
grens	

SOUGHT-AFTER SPATIAL STRUCTURE FOR ANTWERP NORTH EAST AS A RESULT OF,
FOR EXAMPLE, THE SKETCHES FROM THE EXPERIENCE RESEARCH

EXPLORATION INTO THE LIFESTYLE CONCEPT IN HOUSING NEEDS RESEARCH IN FLANDERS

Ann Pisman
University of Ghent (UGent)
Artesis University College of Antwerp
Ann.Pisman@ugent.be, Ann.Pisman@artesis.be
–

Why do people live in a particular location and what do they expect from (the changes in) their housing environment? This research attempts to provide an answer to these generic questions through the intermediary of the lifestyle concept. This concept emphasises increasing social individualisation and the relationship between personally selected patterns of values and activities of (groups of) individuals. The main focus of this research is the hypothesis that a relationship can also be found between the characteristics of the lifestyles of those residents and the characteristics of their current or future housing environments. In order to clarify this hypothesis, quantitative and qualitative research will be performed in (two case areas) in Flanders. Finally, this research is also expected to provide answers which can be used both by private market players as well as by authorities when considering new housing environments or when transforming existing housing environments.

KEYWORDS

Migration, suburbanisation, lifestyles, values, creation and transformation of housing environments.

INTRODUCTION

International literature refers to the increasing individualisation (Crompton, 1998) as one of the significant developments that have brought about drastic changes in society in recent decades. Compared to the past, people are much less reliant on traditional opinions and previously demarcated social categories; they create their own lives instead of following a route mapped out for them. On the housing market, vendors take full advantage of this development. They make it clear to potential buyers that their housing environment helps them to express their own identity and lifestyle. The Durabrik company in Flanders recently offered so-called ECO, DOMO, SILVER and FAMILYhomes[1] for sale, names which no longer simply refer to the features of the homes but rather to the lifestyles of the potential buyers.

According to Chaney, lifestyles are characteristic of modern life and differentiating between lifestyles has therefore become a new and modern way of differentiating between social groups. He also states that *'lifestyles help to make sense of what people do, and why they do it, and what doing it means to them and others'*[2]. Lifestyle research can therefore be used to probe into the underlying motives of consumers.

Finally, Clapham (2005) establishes an explicit link between lifestyles and housing needs by stating that, in postmodern society, housing needs have become detached from the basic human needs but are formed by personally chosen lifestyles. How these new insights, related to individualisation and

[1] According to the company marketing, the four theme homes each focus on a specific area of interest:
-ECO: the environmental aspect (solar panels...)
-DOMO: enjoying wellness and domotics
-SILVER: lifelong housing
-FAMILY: child-friendly home (underfloor heating...)
[2] Chaney D., *Lifestyles*, London, 1996, p.4.

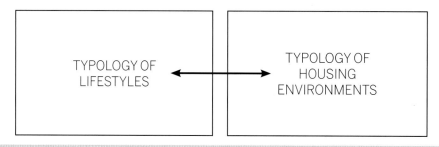

RESEARCH HYPOTHESIS

lifestyles, affect migration patterns in Flanders is as yet unclear. The results from analyses of recent Flemish migration patterns differ greatly. Some speak of an urban *revival*, whereas others point to the steadily increasing suburbanisation of Flanders.

It is within this context that the following main research question is established:

• Why do people live in a particular location and what do they expect from (changes in) their housing environment?

The basic hypothesis of the research is that, on the one hand, there is a relationship between the lifestyles of the residents and, on the other hand, the housing environment in which they (want to) live. People settle in a housing environment which suits their current lifestyle or will transform their housing environment in accordance with their changing lifestyle.

This research topic is very topical in the Flemish planning context. After all, in 1997 the Flemish government approved a policy plan which strongly differentiated between urbanised and rural areas. Going against the current trends of suburbanisation, the Flemish government set itself a target to create 60% of new homes in urban areas, and barely 40% in the Flemish countryside. In 2007, this ambitious target has still not been met. Flemish families still prefer a more rural housing environment. Explanations are sought with regard to the socio-demographic characteristics of these families, but the argument that families with children still opt for quiet, leafy housing environments, only partially seems to stand up in the current ageing and individualising social context.

Finally, in this research new insights are expected as far as living in Flanders is concerned, because for the first time in a Flemish context, links are being sought between housing needs and the psychographic[3] characteristics of the residents. These insights can be used both by private market players as well as by the authorities when considering new housing environments or when transforming existing housing environments.

CONTENT AND SUBJECT

This research will make use of various, complementary research methods.

Achieving a sound scientific basis for this research requires a thorough analysis of the academic literature on the main concept of lifestyles in general, and applications of the lifestyle concept in relation to personal housing expectations. Recent (Flemish) migration and housing needs research will also be examined.

Given that there is currently no lifestyle typology available in Flanders which could serve as the basis for this research, exploratory quantitative research will be performed in order to develop a usable lifestyle typology. An internet survey on lifestyles and housing styles will provide the necessary data for this purpose. Statistical analyses of these data will make it possible to work out a lifestyle typology. The global survey will lift a veil on the diversity in the current values and activities pattern of Flemings.

The main hypothesis of the research will be tested in two case areas in Flanders. In these cases it can be checked to what

3   = related to lifestyles

extent particular groups of Flemings can identify with their own housing environment and what expectations they have for their housing future. The decision has been taken to opt for case study research due to the *why and how questions* which are central in the research set-up (Yin, 2003). Naturally, case study research is limited as far as making general statements is concerned. These case studies therefore tend to fulfil an explorative and descriptive role and focus on underlying explanations for phenomena. The location opted for is a more rural area, *'het Meetjesland'*, and a rather urbanised area, i.e. the City of Ghent including its surrounding areas. The lifestyle survey is repeated with a representative sample of the local population. These results will be confronted with a typology of housing environments yet to be developed. This will require the statistical clustering of data related to physical and social aspects of the housing environments. The hypothesis can be tested on the basis of these quantitative, statistical methods. Interviews with privileged witnesses and land surveys will provide additional insights and explanations for migrations of people or transformations of certain housing environments.

The clear demarcation of the research project results in the following three (sub)research questions:

• Which lifestyle groups, relevant to the housing needs of these groups, can be distinguished in Flanders?

• How do lifestyles and housing environments relate to each other within two sectors in Flanders?

• At Flemish level, how can the concept of lifestyles be integrated into the town planning process of new housing environments and in the transformation of existing housing environments?

RESULTS AND DISCUSSION

The lifestyle concept is a relatively new concept in the academic world of town planning but already has a whole history in sociological research and in marketing research. Naturally, the aim of the research in both disciplines differs completely which is reflected in the way in which the lifestyle concept is approached.

In the sociological discipline, the lifestyle concept is primarily used to describe (the evolution of) social complexity (Weber, Wirth, Bourdieu, Rokeach). Lifestyle groups are being related to standards and values of groups of people within this social context.

Marketing research (Mitchell, Ventura) is primarily associated with consumer-product relationships and therefore tends to focus more on the activities of groups of people. The aim of this research is to gain an insight into consumer behaviour in order to finally achieve a better match between consumer and product.

With regard to the focus on housing, both approaches can be used. In this context, the housing environment can be viewed as a product, which now, but also in the future, must retain a certain appeal for the residents as consumers and users. The future expectations of the residents can additionally be mapped out on the basis of (evolutions of) their standards and values patterns.

For the purpose of the research, a lifestyle group is defined as follows: a lifestyle group is a group of people of similar opinions, standards, values and behaviour.

These insights will serve to compile the survey into the quantitative exploration of the lifestyle concept in Flanders. The survey will both enquire into the global standard and value patterns of the respondents as well as into more specific behaviour patterns or specific value patterns which are directly linked to housing. The main concepts used for the operationalisation of the activities pattern are derived from the literature study of migration and housing needs research in Flanders and are:

• intellectual status/creativity

• economic status

• fear/security

• mobility

• environmental well-being

NEXT STEPS

In the short term, before the end of 2008, the processed survey results will be used to give an answer to the first (sub)research question into the typology of lifestyle groups in Flanders.

Only upon completion of the case studies will it become clear whether the basic hypothesis of this research, that is to say, the relationship between lifestyles on the one hand, and housing needs on the other hand, stands up and in which way these new insights can prove useful to private or government bodies. ■

Ph.D Thesis Directors
Prof. Dr. Georges Allaert (UGent)
Prof. Dr.ir.arch. Piet Lombaerde
Artesis University College of Antwerp

ACKNOWLEDGEMENTS

This research is financed by the Artesis University College of Antwerp.

REFERENCES

Chaney D., *Lifestyles*, London, 1996.

Clapham D., *The meaning of housing. A pathways approach*, Bristol, 2005.

Crompton R., *Class and Stratification. An introduction to Current Debates*, Cambridge, 1998.

Ministerie van de Vlaamse Gemeenschap, *Ruimtelijk Structuurplan Vlaanderen, gecoördineerde versie*, Brussel, 2004.

Yin R. K., *Case study research. Design and methods, applied social research methods*, London, 2003.

SHARED TERMS FOR THE SPATIAL QUALITY OF STRATEGIC PROJECTS

ADS
19/20

Marleen Goethals
Artesis University College of Antwerp
KU Leuven
Marleen.goethals@artesis.be
–

In order to discover the methodologies for determining the quality of a strategic project, literature research is performed into the theories for evaluating the space and into possible frameworks for thought.

The aim of this research is to discover and to refine methodologies which can assist a group of agents to define shared terms (Hajer and Sijmons 2006) for determining the quality of a strategic spatial project so that they can be included into the project definitions. The same shared terms can then also be used as part of the evaluation framework. These methodologies would have to promote the co-production of projects by optimising the quality of the exchange of information which is taking place during the discussions between the agents. This would really have to enable the agents to assist in improving or in maintaining the quality of the space, all the dimensions of spatial quality would have to be considered in the project definition, and it should enrich the quality of the project. Thus, the result should stand a greater chance of being perceived in a positive light by the parties concerned, as well as by the users of the project in spatial planning, environmental psychology, and spatial design theory. The empirical aspect concerns participating observations of concrete 'examplary' processes in the practice of 'strategic projects'. The findings from these cases will then be confronted with the theories concerning the evaluation of space and the operational frameworks from the literature study. These confrontations will then lead to recommendations for approaching strategic projects.

KEYWORDS

Spatial quality, project definition, evaluation framework, designing research, project process, perception of the space.

INTRODUCTION

This research into an operational framework for the spatial quality of strategic spatial projects is part of a series of research projects which is currently being performed within the research group 'Spatial Planning to Strategic Projects'. The research group comprises professors and scientists from the KULeuven, U Gent and the Universiteit Antwerpen.

The aim of the research is to develop an integrated and innovative approach to strategic projects. The topics that will be covered are spatial concept development, innovative policy instruments, process management and management for sustainable development and spatial quality.

This part of the research into an operational framework for spatial quality will be based on the basic premise that the qualities of the space of a strategic project cannot entirely be determined beforehand. They are linked to a spatial and social context. The definition of what spatial quality is in a specific project is the outcome of a complex process in which the participants with differing objectives have to arrive at an agreement (Reijndorp et al. 1998). The sought-after spatial quality can therefore only be defined after the various interests have been considered and have been weighed up against each other (Reijndorp et al. 1998).

- It has been noted that discussions concerning the qualities of a strategic project progress with difficulty due to the fact that the various parties concerned are not absolutely certain what spatial quality exactly stands for. As a result, important aspects of quality, such as the way the space is experienced, is not given sufficient prominence in the comparisons that are made.

- The aim of this research is to discover and refine the methodologies which can help a group of agents to define shared terms (Hajer and Sijmons 2006) in order to determine the quality of a strategic spatial project so that these may be included in the project definitions. The same shared terms can subsequently also be used as part of the evaluation framework. These methodologies can be useful to promote the co-production of projects.

CONTENT

1. GLOBAL SET-UP

The intention is to trace the intended methodologies, which can assist a group of agents to define the shared terms for determining the quality of a strategic project, both in theoretical works as well as in the actual practice of projects. The findings from the theory and the practice would then have to result in recommendations which can be used to develop improved and workable methodologies.

The empirical research consists of participative observations during three different phases of three real project processes. In the course of this research, the literature research largely takes place simultaneously with the empirical research. However, at the start of the research, the literature research did have a headstart. This literature research provided the impetus for a framework for analysis for the participative observations.

The two research questions for this literature research, 'What are the terms used for determining the quality of the space?' and 'How can these terms for determining the quality be shared?' will result in essential information for the methodologies to be developed.

2. THEORETICAL RESEARCH

2.1. What are the terms for determining the quality of the space?

In the Structural plan for Flanders, the concept of spatial quality is understood as 'the evaluation of the space'. Quality in the sense of 'evaluation' expresses a judgement or wish. (...) Therefore, spatial quality is not primarily concerned with the capacity of the object in itself (the intrinsic features of a landscape, of an old city centre, or a municipal space...) but instead the value that is attributed to it. (...). This evaluation is determined both socially and culturally and is therefore time-dependent. (...) By continuing to refine and describe the various criteria, the concept of spatial quality therefore has to be operationalised time and time again (Spatial structural plan for Flanders 1997).

The literature research includes a search for what these various criteria might be.

In the series of theories concerning town planning design (For example, Camillo Sitte, Gordon Cullen, Christopher Alexander, Kevin Lynch), the objectives to strive for to achieve a good environment are both expressed in proposals for new city structures, the fabric of the city, the design of the public space, types of access.. but also in earlier general terms and checklists for good town planning design work. Whereas Cullen and Sitte primarily emphasise the visual experience of a space, the assessment of space in 'A Theory of Good City Form' (Lynch 1981) approaches the topic from various angles (disciplines). According to Lynch, five dimensions, Vitality, Sense, Fit, Access, Control, and two meta-criteria, Efficiency and Justice must enable a group of people to evaluate the space. Different groups will attribute different priorities to these dimensions. As soon as the space is analysed and evaluated on the basis of these dimensions, guidelines can then be drawn up to redevelop existing spaces, or guidelines which result in a necessary spatial intervention for maintaining or increasing the spatial quality.

More recent theories on determining the quality of the space (Oswald & Bacini 2003, Carmona 2004) also approach the space from different angles. In contrast to Lynch, these more

Dimensions of performance		Sustainable urban design principles		Criteria for evaluating Urban Quality in Urban Systems	
Lynch 1982		*Carmona 2004*		*Oswald and Bacini 2003*	
1.	Vitality	1.	Stewardship	1.	Identification
2.	Sense	2.	Resource efficiency	2.	Diversity
3.	Fit	3.	Diversity and choice	3.	Flexibility
4.	Access	4.	Human needs	4.	Degree of self-sufficiency
5.	Control	5.	Resilience	5.	Resource efficiency
		6.	Pollution reduction		
		7.	Concentration		
		8.	Distinctiveness		
		9.	Biotic support		
		10.	Self-sufficiency		

FIGURE 1: THEORIES ON DETERMINING THE QUALITY OF THE SPACE

recent theories are written from a specific municipal model or municipal paradigm. Carmona starts from models for sustainable urban design, and Oswald & Bacini from the model of the so-called network city, rasterstad or Netzstadt.

Lynch's theory is applicable to various city models. Even though his 'dimensions of performance' are directly linked to space, they do not dictate any specific design solutions. Thus, one of the 'dimensions of performance', 'Sense' in particular, is very well worked out. Using a number of subdimensions for 'Sense', Lynch endeavours to fathom out why people feel so good in a particular space, and why such a space can have an emotionally and inspirational effect on people.

Given that Lynch's theory is based on human values and needs, and consists of dimensions which can be refined differently depending on the project, this theory (for the time being) is the most suitable to meet 'the criteria to be refined for evaluating an environment' (RSV 1997) for which we are searching.

In research which dates back to 2000, M.H. Jacobs also states that in our society various disciplines are debated and that meaning is given to the concept of 'quality living environment'. In order to link the various disciplines which in one way or another are preoccupied with the quality of the living environment, he created a framework for thought for the quality of the living environment. For the purpose of this link he bases himself on the Pirsig analysis of needs. Quality is subdivided into four levels, the biological, the social, the psychical and the metaphysical level (Jacobs 2000).

Besides the literature on design theory, the literature from the disciplines of spatial planning and environmental psychology (Cooper Marcus, C., Francis, C. Kaplan, R. & Kaplan, S. & Ryan, R.) has also been explored.

2.2. How can the terms for determining quality be shared?

Bringing about spatial quality in strategic spatial projects requires good communication with regard to that spatial quality (Schreurs in Geldof (ed.) 2005).

As a methodology to assist a group of agents in defining the indicators for quality of the public space, Jan Schreurs proposes a 'Framework for discussion concerning the indicators for the quality of the public space' (Schreurs 2007). It is a theoretical discussion tool to weigh up the various interests and various quality facets against each other. This matrix also monitors

ADS
19/20

Level	Biological	Social	Psychical	Metaphysical
Disciplines	β sciences - geology - hydrology - environmental science - ecology - biology - physiology	γ sciences - economy - sociology - cultural anthropology	α sciences - psychology - phenomenology	- religion - art - philosophy
Dominant processes in the Human-Environment relationship	Biological and physiological processes	Automatisms, customs, transferred behaviour, role models	Conscious choices, awareness of the here and now, self-actualisation	Self-contemplation and the here and now in the light of all that is possible
Determinants	Laws	Rules	Strategies	Ideals

FIGURE 2: CONCEPTUAL FRAMEWORK QUALITY (JACOBS 2000)

that all of the quality dimensions (Lynch 1984) are considered. Kaplan, Kaplan & Ryan provide a few interesting insights into communicating about the quality of space design. There are bits and pieces of relevant information in many people's heads. In order to share this information among the various parties, there must be an **exchange of information**. This process has more chance of succeeding if one takes into account the 'mental maps' of the various recipients of information.

Such maps are developed separately for each individual. It is a long-winded process determined by education, training, and experience. The 'mental map' determines how an individual judges the space.

Experts, as a result of their training and experience, have developed a way of perceiving which differs profoundly from how citizens look at things. It is characteristic of experts that they do not realise that their perception of a situation differs strongly from the perceptions of those who do not have this expertise. (For example, a photographer sees an environment in terms of light, a real estate developer thinks of real estate prices, and a designer has an eye for circulation patterns.) (Kaplan, Kaplan & Ryan 1998).

2.3. Research Questions for Case Analyses

The literature research results in a provisional description of a number of concepts that are crucial to the research and a series of research questions for the case analyses.

1. Are all of Lynch's 'dimensions of performance' taken into consideration in the discussions?
2. Which terms are used (words or images) by the various parties to communicate? To what degree are they determined by the interests they pursue or by the training and experience of the agent?
3. How are the dimensions refined in his work?
4. What role does designing research play in the process that leads to the sharing of terms?
5. During the process, does one build up a project specific framework for consideration? Which are the similarities and differences with Schreurs's framework for discussion?
6. Which structure for discussion makes it possible to share terms in the course of the project?
7. How does one organise the exchange of information?

MATRIX		INTERESTS				
		SOCIAL	CULTURAL	ECONOMIC	ECOLOGICAL	INSTITUTIONAL
VALUES	VITALITY					
	SENSE					
	FIT					
	ACCESS					
	CONTROL					

FIGURE 3: SCHREURS'S THEORETICAL DISCUSSION TOOL (SCHREURS 2007)

3. EMPIRICAL RESEARCH

3.1. Methodology

Three phases from three different project processes will be observed. The researcher has been involved in each project in a professional capacity.

- In the case of the Oosterweel junction, the researcher has been a member of the design team for one of the three competing consortiums since the end of 2005.
- In the Case process 'Masterplan public space Gentse torenrij', the researcher acted from September 2007 until the end of December 2007 as a sounding board for the design team Robbrecht and Daem and M. José Van Hee Architecten.
- The Case 'City Renovation Project Roeselare Central' is a concept subsidy project for Flemish city policy. This case runs from January until September 2008 and will be observed as a participating 'local consultant concept subsidisation' appointed by the public works team for Flemish city policy.

In those various capacities, the researcher can observe discussions between various categories of agents, for example, discussions with members of the quality chamber, discussions with users and groups of residents, discussions between contractors and designers, discussions at meetings of aldermen, consultancy groups....

Furthermore, in all cases, interviews with key figures are being recorded, and written sources, such as project definitions, reports from panels of judges, press articles and websites of action groups are being analysed.

CONCLUSIONS

The factors, which according to the literature research determine terminology sharing for the purpose of determining the spatial quality of a project, can also be identified in the empirical research. For example, below we have briefly described two sets of findings from a more extensive series.

- The terms which crop up during discussions, or in written sources, can always be described as refinements, actualisations of Lynch's five 'dimensions of performance'. However, the terms do not always occur simultaneously. In the case of the 'Master Plan for Public Open Space Gentse Torenrij', the initial stage only paid attention to 'Sense' and 'Access'. By introducing new agents into the discussions, the safety factor was also added (actualisation of 'Vitality'). Each agent views the project from their own personal 'mental map' (Kaplan, Kaplan & Ryan 1998). The angles from which the various agents approach the project are therefore deeply determined by their training and the interests which they pursue. In this sense, the combination of agents participating in a process will determine the completeness of the terms which will be weighed up, and therefore the riches of the shared terminology which will be decided upon.
- Another finding in the Ghent case is that participation in a process of intensive exchange of information (research, designing research, discussions, etc.) develops a 'shared mental map' among the agents. The agents then hold a number of common images and insights concerning the project.

However, this requires an efficient exchange of information. This case has demonstrated that the variants actualised by the designing research for the public transport stop configuration promote the exchange of information and make it more accurate. On the basis of input provided by the agents, it was possible to develop a third variant which combines the advantages of both previous suggestions.

The intention is to draw up a proposal of recommendations for each project which can optimise the methodology applied for the sharing of terms. These recommendations will subsequently be submitted to the main agents of the projects observed. The comments from these agents will then be processed into the final recommendations. ■

Ph.D Thesis Director
Prof. Dr.ir.arch. Jan Schreurs
KU Leuven

REFERENCES

Alexander, C. 1977 *A Pattern Language,* London: John Willey & Sons

Carmona, M. and Sieh, L. 2004 *Measuring Quality in planning. Managing the performance process,* London and New York: Spon Press

Collins, G. and Collins, C. 1986 *Camillo Sitte: The Birth of Modern City Planning (with a translation of the 1889 Austrian edition of his City Planning according to Artistic Principles),* New York: Rizzoli

Cooper Marcus, C., Francis, C. 1998 *People places second edition Design Guidelines for Urban Open Space,* New York: John Wiley & Sons, inc.

Hajer, M. en Sijmons, D. 2006 *Een plan dat werkt. Ontwerp en politiek in de regionale planvorming,* Rotterdam: NAi Uitgevers

Jacobs, M.H., 2000 *Kwaliteit leefomgeving, Kennisontwikkeling,* Wageningen: Alterra, Research Instituut voor de Groene Ruimte

Kaplan, R. & Kaplan, S. & Ryan, R. 1998 *With People in Mind. Design and Management of Everyday Nature,* Washington, D.C.: Island Press

Lynch, K. 1984 *Good City Form,* Massachusetts: Massachusetts Institute of Technology

Oswald, F. and Bacini, P. 2003 *Netzstadt. Designing the urban,* Basel, Boston, Berlin: Birkhäuser

Reijndorp, A., Truijens, B., Nio, I., Visser, H., Kompier, V. 1998 *De kern van het ruimtelijk beleid. Een onderzoek naar het begrip ruimtelijke kwaliteit,* Den Haag: Wetenschappelijke Raad voor het Regeringsbeleid

Schreurs, J. in Geldof, M., Laenen, K., Schreurs, J., Stuyven, K., et al. (ed.) 2005 *Ruimtelijke kwaliteit aan de kust. Indicatoren voor de ruimtelijke kwaliteit van de publieke ruimte en de architectuur aan de kust,* Brussel: Vlaamse Gemeenschap

Schreurs, J. and Martens, M. 2005 *Research by Design as Quality Enhancement,* paper AESOP 05 Vienna

Schreurs, J. 2007 *Communicating Quality: Words and Images,* paper for Quality Conference at the Welsh School of Architecture Cardiff 4-6 Juli 2007

Sternberg, E. 2000 *An Integrative Theory of Urban Design,* APA Journal, Summer 2000, Vol. 66, No. 3

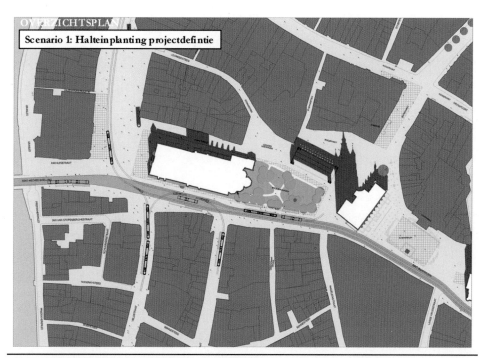

Robbrecht en Daem, M. José Van Hee Architecten en Technum

SCENARIO 1: PROJECT DEFINITION FOR PUBLIC TRANSPORT STOP LAYOUT

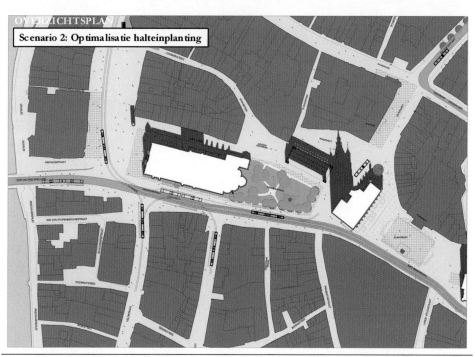

Robbrecht en Daem, M. José Van Hee Architecten en Technum

SCENARIO 2: OPTIMISATION OF PUBLIC TRANSPORT STOP LAYOUT

ADS
19/20

LANDSCAPE PLANNING FOR URBAN NETWORKS

David Verhoestraete
Artesis University College of Antwerp
david.verhoestraete@artesis.be
—

The core economic area of Western Europe is characterised by some typical examples of urban networks: the Flemish Diamond, the Ruhr-area and the Randstad-area. Each of these regions consists of several networks of small scaled interrelated urban centres instead of one metropolitan area. The ongoing urbanisation process within these network cities creates a low building density. The remaining fragments of open space are characterised by intensive land use as a result of the limited available space, as opposed to the typical underutilization of the hinterland of most metropolises.

The dominant policy within the network city focuses on zoning and protecting the remaining open space in nature conservation areas, water collecting areas, agricultural areas, etc. This approach has two important disadvantages. Firstly, the sectoral needs and the underlying perspectives are hardly achieved (e.g. numerous nature conservation areas are not located on the hot spots of biodiversity, but rather on remaining spaces which are economically less interesting for other purposes). Secondly, the sectoral approach leads to the juxtaposition of highly intensive monofunctional fragments consuming more space than multiple land use with extensive interrelating functions.

Therefore, landscape planning in urban networks demands a specific approach.
This PhD research focuses on two complementary approaches. The first approach explores the possibilities of implementing the concept of *ecosystem services* in the spatial planning policy. Ecosystem services are the benefits people obtain from ecosystems. These include provisioning services such as food and water; regulating services such as regulation of floods, drought and land degradation; supporting services such as soil formation and nutrient cycling, and cultural services such as recreational benefits. The second approach explores the possibilities of a *programmatic intensification* of the open space by converting sectoral needs and zones into specific environmental conditions as common denominators for the formerly conflicting land use claims (water quality, building density, accessibility, biodiversity). The overlay of these specific environmental conditions results in a multifunctional landscape with different spatial development perspectives.

KEYWORDS

Landscape planning, urban networks, ecosystem services, multifunctional landscapes ■

Ph.D Thesis Directors
Prof. dr. Patrick Meire
Ecosystem Management Research Group, University of Antwerp
Prof. dr. Richard Foqué
Artesis University College of Antwerp
Dr. Hans Leinfelder
Centre for Mobility and Physical Planning, Ghent University

CONSTRUCTION, TECHNOLOGY AND MATERIALS IN THE JESUIT CHURCHES IN THE LOW COUNTRIES

Els Van Hamme
Artesis University College of Antwerp
els.vanhamme@artesis.be
–

The study focuses on constructive and technical aspects of the Jesuit churches in the Low Countries, as well as on the use of materials. The technical aspects are related to the evolution of sciences – and thus the theoretical knowledge – in the Low Countries during the sixteenth and seventeenth centuries.

In our regions Baroque architecture was confined at first to ornamental details. Which Jesuit churches show a Baroque construction and to what extent? Where does the background from the architects come into this? Roman examples are confronted with case studies from the Southern Netherlands. Much has been written on Baroque architecture, but aspects of construction, technology and use of materials are still open for investigation.

KEYWORDS

Building construction, Construction materials, Construction methods, processes and tools, Relation between empiricism and science in construction

INTRODUCTION

The society of Jesus, established by Saint Ignatius of Loyola in 1539, played an important role in the revival of the Catholic faith, following the Council of Trent. In the Low Countries, the period under the reign of the archdukes Albrecht and Isabella was very productive for the Jesuits: in a period of Counter-Reformation, the new religious orders enjoyed the support of the Archdukes. The Jesuits benefited the most, which allowed them to complete their ambitious building programmes. The Archdukes also contributed to the expansion of the Baroque architecture in the Low Countries, since they preferred architects who had acquired experience in Italy. The major need for colleges, churches and schools made it impossible for the Jesuits to distribute all the assignments to members of the Society. When non-Jesuits were appointed, the Royal architects were "lent out" to the Jesuits.

In Italy, the influence of Renaissance and Baroque architecture was felt in two areas: the architectural design and the way of constructing. The Low Countries, however, had a much stronger tradition in Gothic architecture than Italy, and so it took a lot longer before the new ways of constructing were imported here. In the beginning, the influence of the Baroque was confined to ornamental details.

To acquire a better understanding of the way of building, we have to learn which level of technical and scientific knowledge the architects and builders of this period possessed. Nowadays great structures are calculated in advance to maintain stability, but until the Renaissance period, constructing large buildings was a process of trial and error, for the architects, engineers and craftsman had to rely on intuition and experience. The constructive problems the builders had to deal with were related to theoretical knowledge.

The essence of the research can be summarised in three questions:

ST. LOUP. BARREL VAULT

- What is new for the early baroque in the Low Countries with regard to constructive and technical aspects?
- Which aspects of construction were renewed under the influence of Baroque architecture? Domes, foundations, spans, trusses, materials, etc.. For which elements did the builders hold on to traditional methods?
- Which were the influences by which Baroque architecture penetrated in the Low Countries? Because the (Jesuit) architects from the 16th and 17th centuries had the possibility to make study tours, influences from other countries could more easily set in. Besides Italian influences, were there also aspects from French or English Baroque visible?

CONTENT AND SUBJECT

To get started with the research a status questionis had to be made about constructing Jesuit churches in the Low Countries and about construction and technology. The first part of the research thus embraced the study of literature and resources.

It was important to make a choice of the case studies as soon as possible, because it allowed a much more specific approach.

For the case studies, the churches with a "Baroque" construction method – or where at least a part of the construction followed the new, Italian way of construction – were taken into consideration.

ST. CHARLES BORROMEO. TOWER © P. LOMBAERDE

The four chosen churches are fine examples of all kinds of structural problems the architects and builders had to deal with, but they also show us the evolution in constructing Jesuit churches from the beginning until the end of the 17th century in the Low Countries.

The Jesuit church in Antwerp (currently St. Charles Borromeo) was designed by father François de Aguilón. After his death in 1617 lay-brother Huyssens took over. The church was built between 1615 and 1621. For this study, an investigation of the foundations is interesting, because the church is built over a canal. The recent restoration of the tower brought up some interesting constructional details, such as the use of tie-rods in the tower.

The old Jesuit church Saint Ignatius, nowadays Saint Loup, in Namur, was designed by lay-brother Huyssens. The church was built between 1621 and 1645. The roof structure of this church is worthy of investigation: the barrel vault is connected to the roof truss by means of iron tie-rods, which are tied up in the masonry of the outer walls. Also the barrel vault in the middle aisle is very rare in the Low Countries.

With regard to the construction of domes, the St. Michael church in Leuven was chosen. This Jesuit church was originally meant to be a domed church, with the cupola on the crossing of transept and choir. However, during construction, the supports turned out to be insufficient and so the church ended up without a dome. The drawings kept in the *Promptuarium Pictorum* give a good idea of the original design Willem Hesius

ST. MICHAEL (LEUVEN). INTERIOR VIEW OF THE FRONT FACADE
SOURCE: PROMPTUARIUM PICTORUM

thought of. The church was built between 1650 and 1666.

The original drawings for the St-Francis-Xavier church, currently the St. Pieter and Paulus church, in Mechelen, are also kept in the *Promptuarium Pictorum* and show a lot of structural details that are worthy of investigation. This church was designed by Antoine Losson and built between 1670 and 1677.

For this part of the research two paths will be followed. First, a very specific bibliography has to be made for each case study, always with regard to the constructive and technical aspects. This bibliography is important in order to obtain as much information about the subject as possible. But, since the resources regarding constructive and technical aspects are rather limited, a second aspect of the research is to investigate the case studies on site as well.

At the same time, the problems the architects and builders had to deal with during the design and construction process, can also be investigated in two ways. First of all, the problems that occurred have to be studied in the context of that specific case study. How did the architect (with his specific background) solve the problem? How did the problem come about in the first place? A second step in this part of the study will be to examine the problem theoretically.

When the study of the four chosen churches and their problems will be finished, the results can be compared with foreign examples. Did the architects and builders from different countries use different solutions for the same problems? Again this is related to the knowledge of the architects and builders in the different countries.

RESULTS AND DISCUSSION

Surprisingly little is known about the constructive and technical aspects of the baroque churches. This aspect of the baroque period is therefore still open for investigation.

The goal is to obtain more information and a better notion of the construction of the four chosen case studies in the first place, and then see them in the bigger picture, meaning the Jesuit churches from the 16th and 17th century.

I hope to acquire a clearer view of how information and knowledge between architects and builders of different

54

countries and with different backgrounds and education was passed on.

CONCLUSION

Currently I am investigating the first case study: St. Charles Borromeo in Antwerp.

As mentioned earlier, the purpose is to investigate all four case studies by literature and on site as well.

Later on, they can be compared with foreign examples. ∎

Ph.D Thesis Directors
Prof.dr.ir.arch. Piet Lombaerde
University of Antwerp
Artesis University College of Antwerp
Prof. Dr. Guido Marnef
University of Antwerp

REFERENCES

Daelemans B., *Het Promptuarium Pictorum Volume II. Een studie van barokke architectuur-tekeningen uit de zuidelijke Nederlanden*, (onuitgegeven licentiaatsverhandeling KUL), Leuven,1998

De Jonge K., De Vos A., *Bellissimi ingegni, grandissimo splendore: studies over de religieuze architectuur in de Zuidelijke Nederlanden tijdens de 17de eeuw*, Leuven, 2000

Lemmens S., *Onderzoek naar de theoretische kennis en de ontwerppraktijk binnen de architecturale entourage van de jezuïetenorde in de 16de en 17de eeuw in de provinvie Flandro-Belgica*, (onuitgegeven licentiaatsverhandeling KUL), Leuven, 1996

Parsons W.B., *Engineers and engineering in the Renaissance*, Cambridge, 1976.

Plantenga J.H., *L'architecture religieuse dans l'ancien Duché de Brabant depuis le règne des archiducs jusqu'au gouvernement autrichien*, Den Haag, 1926C. Singer; E.J. Holmyard, *A History of Technology*, (5 vol.), Londen, 1957.

Wittkower R., Jaffe I.B., *Baroque Art. The Jesuit Contribution*, New York, 1972.

Ziggelaar A., *François de Aguilon (1567-1617): scientist and architect*, Institutum Historicum, Rome, 1983.

ST. PIETER AND PAULUS (MECHELEN). SECTION
SOURCE: PROMPTUARIUM PICTORUM

ADS
19/20

RESEARCH INTO THE RELATIONSHIP BETWEEN CITY DESIGN AND URBAN THEORY IN A NUMBER OF CITIES IN THE LOW COUNTRIES (1576-1660)

Jochen De Vylder
Artesis University College of Antwerp
jochen.devylder@artesis.be
–

The topic of this doctoral research consists of a comparison between a series of cities from the Low Countries for the period 1576-1660, the aim of which is to discern the effect of the general theoretical and idealising treatises in relation to the actual reality of city design in order to gain an insight into the morphological and typological transformations both within a specific physico-spatial constellation as well as within a short-term and long-term historical friction. A powerful example is the rubbing along of the temporal and spatial strata in the case of the redesign of 'monastery grounds' as the superposition of a topological and morphological order, or in accordance with the order of the treaties.

The hypothesis is based upon the provisional assessment that the city designs itself. This means that the more implicit strategies within the confrontation between treatise and city design determine the reality of the city and therefore makes the content and methodology of the treatise and the design less relative.

KEYWORDS

Architecture Theory, Urbanism, Design strategy

INTRODUCTION

The content of this thesis examines the interaction between the treatise on the ideal city and city design with its actual parcellation, resulting in municipal and physico-spatial transformation processes which take place over extended periods of time. It covers a discourse which as a consequence of the application of various concepts leads to both a physico-spatial result as well as to a transformation of the type of 'long term' event. Within the aforementioned interaction, the specific periods in the city history and in its treatises as well as the various innovations constitute the starting-points for the research.

The basic hypothesis of this research is that theory - in the form of treatises - undeniably has an impact on the city design method and its municipal interventions. Vice versa, city design offers resistance by advancing its historical reality at particular times and at specific locations with as a result that the theory itself transforms itself or is forced to make new statements. The manner in which this social production has led to innovations in town planning practice will have to be examined and the hypothesis is that it is a question here of short and long-term strategies. Furthermore, the issue is the ground-breaking nature of the research, this in contrast to many other - unfortunately less speculative - studies (Ed

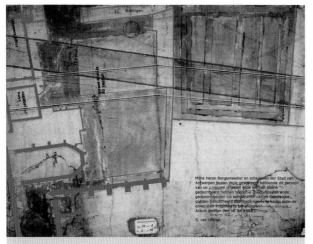
PROPOSITION FOR A STREET THROUGH THE DOMINICAN CONVENT
(REPRESENTED IN RED), ANTWERP. 1582 (SA:ICO 03-16B)

Taverne, Charles van den Heuvel et al.), which link the changes in the Netherlands primarily to large-scale city expansion, the creation of new cities or the construction of new fortifications based on fortified city walls. In this doctoral study, the focus is in the first instance aimed at often the more modest but also more conceptual transformation processes in the historical city. The central items of research in this thesis are, on the one hand, the design drawings, sometimes accompanied by manifesto documents, which cover the topic of the reallocated use or transformation of the confiscated monastery estates and other clerical properties and the treatises on the ideal city. The main focus of the hypothesis is that on the released monastery estates, which reflect a medieval tradition and are determined topologically, and the city infill in the 1576-1660

PLANPROJECTION OF THE IN 1655 CONSTRUCTED TOWNHALL OF AMSTERDAM . THE BUILDINGBLOCKS IN RED REPRESENT THE SITUATION BEFORE THE
CONSTRUCTION OF THIS TOWNHALL, THE RED HATCHED ZONES REPRESENT THE ERASED CLERICAL PLOTS 'T ELENDIGE KERCK HOFF' AND 'T GASTHUIJS'

period, two eras are rubbing along as three urban concepts, that is to say: a topological, a morphological and an idealistic concept. In order to gain a real insight, both the city design and the treatise are confronted with each other both in language and in drawing.

Inherent to the previously mentioned interaction between treatise and city design, the research does not primarily look into the question already established with regard to implementation of theory into practice but it concerns the question as to how this interaction itself can be acknowledged as a dialectical method and clarified as a strategy. For this reason it is important to examine the importance of the instrument of city design both from the point of view of the language and the formal strata of the city and to objectify the interpretations contained within. The analyses are embedded into the current theories and design strategies of the city in accordance with Aldo Rossi, Colin Rowe, Bernardo Secchi and Rem Koolhaas.

CONTENT AND SUBJECT

After establishing the cities (Antwerp, Ghent, Amsterdam, Leiden, Utrecht) on the basis of available archive material, a number of case studies were selected within the fabric of these cities which profile the mutual differences with regard to the theory formation to be assessed. This choice was made on the basis of an expected tension which arises between, on the one hand, the newly designed fabric and the architecture, and on the other hand, supported by the ideas of the planned mathematical ideal city (both formal as well as contentual) and the existing 'medieval' and less rigid, topological, planned city fabric.

The archives that were found include, on the one hand, designs with as subject the transformation of monastery grounds, and on the other hand, historical city drawings, and these have subsequently been subjected to a formal and structural analysis. The formal research studies the morphological qualities (typo-morphological and topological research) of the various designs and examines them within their spatial context with the assistance of digital processing programs, such as GIS software, and in the historical context. This component also

SAINT VEERLE SQUARE IN GENT. FACADES OF 5 HOUSES (ORIGINALLY 9) BUILT IN 1581 BY SER LIPPENS ON THE GROUNDS OF THE DEMOLISHED SAINT PHALAÏDE CHURCH

highlights a semiotic analysis into the interpretation of the various concepts, such as 'ornament' [sieraet], 'commodity' [commoditeyt], 'profit' [profijt] which occur in the associated explanatory writings. The structural section covers the synchronous and diachronous phenomena in the cities in relation to the thesis. From an adequate list of literature which was carefully focused on the subject matter, an interpretive framework was established in parallel but independently from the case studies, based on the city theories and design strategies of Colin Rowe, Aldo Rossi and Rem Koolhaas and linked to the insights of Gilles Deleuze in order to prepare an external reflective argumentation.

At the end of 2008, the first interpretative statements are expected as a result of comparing the intrinsic theory formation and the interpretative framework in order to compile them, in the course of 2009, into an objectified but ground-breaking argument to provide the foundations for the final thesis.

results and discussion

The material researched has shown that, for the cities Antwerp, Amsterdam and Leiden, the transformation of monastery grounds was almost always linked to the three basic notions (Venustas, Commoditas and Utilitas) which, according to the theoreticians since Alberti, architecture and town planning had to comply with. However, these concepts received a richer, broader and sometimes adjusted significance as a result of the confrontation between the implementation of the rigid theory of the ideal city supported by scientific discoveries, mathesis and the specific topological particular monastery grounds. On the scale of the grounds, the tension between the architecture in situ and the rational implementation is apparent, but the actual design strategies which arise from the dialectic between theory and the existing network are the most obvious on the scale of the city as a whole. Provisional results from a number of case studies demonstrate that not only does a practical physico-spatial link arise between the various small-sale interventions but also an aesthetic and ideological link. The experiments in Antwerp in the last quarter of the sixteenth century can again be detected in city renovations in the Northern Netherlands and their translation in the treatise on architecture and town planning by Simon Stevin. ■

Ph.D Thesis Directors
Prof. Dr.ir.arch. Piet Lombaerde
University of Antwerp
Artesis University College of Antweerp
Prof. Dr.ir.Gerard van Zeijl
Technische Universiteit Eindhoven

REFERENCES

Deleuze G. en Guattari F., *Mille Plateaux*, Parijs, 1980.

Heuvel C. van den, *'Papiere bolwercken': de introductie van de Italiaanse stede- en vestingbouw in de Nederlanden (1540-1609) en het gebruik van tekeningen*, Alphen aan den Rijn, 1991.

Heuvel C. van den, *'De Huysbou'*, A reconstruction of an unfinished treatise on architecture, town planning and civil engineering by Simon Stevin, (History of science and scholarship in the Netherlands, volume 7), KNAW-Edita, Amsterdam, 2005.

Koolhaas R., *Delirious New York*, Rotterdam, 1994.

Koster E.A., *Stadsmorfologie: een proeve van vormgericht onderzoek ten behoeve van stedenbouwhistorisch onderzoek*, Groningen, 2001.

Lombaerde P., 'Continuïteit, vernieuwingen en verschillen: het concept van de stad in de Noordelijke en Zuidelijke Nederlanden rond 1600', in: *Bulletin Knob*, 1999-5/6 (1999), p. 237-248.

Rowe C. and Koetter F., *Collage City*, Cambridge (Mass.), 1978.

Rossi A., *De Architectuur van de stad*, Maastricht, 2002.

Taverne E., *In 't land van belofte: in de nieue stadt: ideaal en werkelijkheid van de stadsuitleg in de Republiek, 1580-1680*, Maarssen, 1978.

Vylder J. 'De, 'Typo-morphological studies: morphological research into the re-use of confiscated land located in cities in the Low Countries: case study Antwerp, during the Calvinist administration, 1577-1585', in: *'The European City': Architectural interventions and Urban Transformations*, Delft, 2005.

RECONSTRUCTED GISMAP OF THE WALLED TOWN OF UTRECHT WITH IN RED REPRESENTED ALL STREETS PROJECTED
ON CLERICAL GROUNDS FOR THE PERIOD 1578-1660

ADS
19/20

ROLE AND MEANING OF DAYLIGHT IN BAROQUE ARCHITECTURE IN WESTERN EUROPE (17TH CENTURY-MIDDLE OF THE 18TH CENTURY)

Nathalie Poppe
Artesis University College of Antwerp
nathalie.poppe@artesis.be

During the 17th and 18th centuries, a scientific revolution flooded Europe. More than ever before, applied sciences gained ground. Experimental research laid the foundation of new ideas and achievements, which were also eagerly used in other fields. In no time, science and arts went hand in hand and caused intellectual tours de force in many disciplines. Likewise, experiments with perspective, geometry and optics influenced architecture. My research investigates the way in which Baroque architects used their knowledge of the action of light in Baroque churches. To that end, a few case studies were chosen, based on historical source investigation. These case studies will be subjected to a digital light study in Ecotect to demonstrate the interaction between the scientific writings of the 17th-18th centuries and the action of light in the architecture of that period.[1]

KEYWORDS

Baroque architecture, scientific writings, churches, optics, action of light.

INTRODUCTION

My research on the action of light in Baroque churches and its relation with scientific writings of that time will be worked out on the basis of three important case studies: the Antwerp St.-Carolus Borromeuschurch (Belgium), the San Lorenzo church of Turin (Italy), and the church of Vierzehnheiligen in Bad Staffelstein (Germany).[2] (figures 1-2-3) A large part of the first case study was treated in my Masters' thesis (2005).[3] The research on the Antwerp church already demonstrated a relationship between scientific writings of the architect himself and his contemporaries and the sophisticated church design. Everything indicates that this Antwerp church is not an isolated example of a cunning architecture in which scientific experiments with optics play an important role. Profound analyses of other case studies could enlighten this issue. Furthermore, digital study allows us to clearly establish the relationship between scientific writings and the action of light in Baroque architecture, based on a whole new approach.

---

1   Ecotect is a software package developed by Australian company Square One Research. Ecotect is a complete building design and environmental analysis tool that covers the broad range of simulation and analysis functions required to truly understand how a building design will operate and perform. (www.squ1.com)

2   Important books on these case-studies are :
    P.LOMBAERDE (ed.), *Innovation and experience in the Early Baroque in the Southern Netherlands. The case of the Jesuit Church of Antwerp*, (Architettura Moderna 6), Turnhout 2008.
    G.DARDANELLO, S. KAIBER and H.A.MILLON, *Guarino Guarini*, Turin 2006.
    P.RUDERICH, *Vierzehnheiligen. Eine Baumonographie*, Bamberg 2000.
3   N.POPPE, *Lichtwerking in de St.-Carolus Borromeus*, Antwerpen 2004-2005.

THE ST.-CAROLUS BORROMEUSCHURCH IN ANTWERP

THE CHURCH OF SAN LORENZO IN TURIN

CONTENT AND SUBJECT

As already mentioned in the introduction, the main research method of my study is based on two important methods of investigation. On the one hand, a large historical source study was necessary. On the other hand, a digital light study was applied to investigate the subject in a whole new way.

Each of the case studies is treated identically, based on the main research method above. The historical study is divided into 2 parts. First of all, research is made on the spirit of the age and scientific evolution. Secondly, an in-depth study is made on the architect(s) of each case study. What was his/their background? What do we know about his/their scientific and artistic interests? Did the architect(s) write down some theories? All of this is necessary to understand the architecture of each case study. In Antwerp, for instance, 3 persons were involved in the design and construction of the Jesuit church: Peter Huyssens, François De Aguilón and Peter Paul Rubens. The last two both wrote an important treatise. Peter Paul Rubens published his *Palazzi di Genova*, a book on the new Italian style, in 1622 in Antwerp.[4],while François De Aguilón published his *Opicorum Libri VI philosophis iuxta ac*

mathematics utiles in 1613.[5] A voluminous work, made up of 6 books, mutually divided by drawings of Peter Paul Rubens. Although De Aguilón's work is mainly based on mathematics, the title of this treatise unites for the first time in history physics, mathematics and philosophy under one science: Optics. Important parts of it consist of hypotheses and experiments. Both works had a great influence on the development of the Antwerp church.

For the case study on the church of San Lorenzo (Turin), the writings of its architect Guarino Guarini are of the same importance to understand not only his architecture, but also that of Balthasar Neumann, architect of the church of Vierzehnheiligen.[6]

These studies on the historical background of each case study are necessary to perform the actual light study. First, an empirical study is made on the daylight in the interior of each church. This empirical study makes it possible to presuppose some hypotheses that can be investigated in the digital light study with *Ecotect*, a software package that allows light division to be examined in great detail. Likewise, in the Antwerp case study, I studied the influence of the bevelled window sills in the

4   See also :
    P.LOMBAERDE (ed.), *The Reception of P.P. Rubens's Palazzi di Genova during the 17th century in Europe: questions and problems*, (Architectura Moderna,1), Turnhout 2002.

5   See also :
    A.ZIGGELAAR, *François De Aguilon s.j. (1567-1617) scientist and architect*, Rome 1983.
6   G.GUARINI, *Architettura Civile*, Turin 1737.

ADS
19/20

side-aisles on the action of light in the church. Also the play of diffuse and direct light was investigated (figures 4-5), because these types of light are the leading figures of a Baroque play of light by which the architects tried to reunite the human and the divine. Two golden rules were applied. First of all, daylight was only allowed to descend where it was meant to, in such a way that it completed the architecture and decoration, greatly contributing to the overall picture. Practically speaking, daylight was meant to illuminate the special parts of the interior (altar, paintings, sculptures...). As a second condition, daylight was not supposed to distract the visitor from what he needed to see. The main method used to satisfy these two conditions, consisted in the use of diffuse and direct light. Important windows were often hidden behind pillars or statues to enlarge the effect of surprise.

The results of the digital light study can only be understood by comparison with the results of the other case studies, measured by the spirit of the age and historical background.

results and discussion

As I already made some important findings for the case study of the Antwerp St.-Carolus Borromeuskerk, I am convinced to find even more astonishing results on the relationship between the scientific writings at the time and Baroque architecture in the other case studies. This will not only improve our understanding of Baroque architecture in general, but will also enlighten the vision on the Baroque spirit of the case studies themselves.

CONCLUSION

I am now working on the case study of the San Lorenzo church in Turin of Guarino Guarini which is also important to understand the architecture of the church of Vierzehnheiligen in Bad Staffelstein from Balthasar Neumann. ∎

Ph.D Directors
prof.dr.ir.arch. Piet Lombaerde
University of Antwerp
Artesis University College of Antwerp
prof.dr. Guido Marnef
University of Antwerp
prof.msc. Marc Muylle
Artesis University College of Antwerp

THE CHURCH OF VIERZEHNHEILIGEN IN BAD STAFFELSTEIN

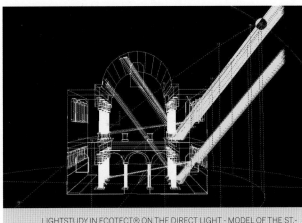

LIGHTSTUDY IN ECOTECT® ON THE DIRECT LIGHT - MODEL OF THE ST.-CAROLUS BORROMEUSCHURCH ON THE 21TH OF APRIL AT 3PM

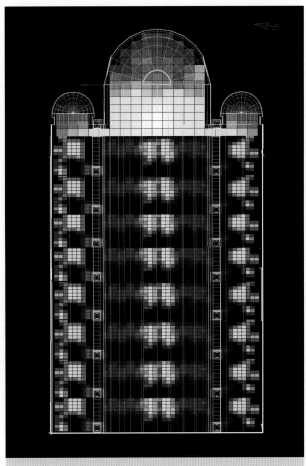

LIGHTSTUDY IN ECOTECT® ON THE DIFFUSE LIGHT - MODEL OF THE ST-CAROLUS BORROMEUSCHURCH ON THE 21TH OF APRIL AT 3PM

REFERENCES

DARDANELLO G., KAIBER S. and MILLON A.H., *Guarino Guarini*, Turin 2006.

GUARINI G., *Architettura Civile*, Turin 1737.

LOMBAERDE P. (ed.), *The Reception of P.P. Rubens's* Palazzi di Genova *during the 17th century in Europe: questions and problems*, (Architectura Moderna,1), Turnhout 2002.

LOMBAERDE P. (ed.), *Innovation and experience in the Early Baroque in the Southern Netherlands. The case of the Jesuit Church of Antwerp*, (Architectura Moderna 6), Turnhout 2008.

POPPE N., *Lichtwerking in de St.-Carolus Borromeus*, Antwerpen 2004-2005.

RUDERICH P., *Vierzehnheiligen. Eine Baumonographie*, Bamberg 2000.

ZIGGELAAR A., *François De Aguilon s.j. (1567-1617) scientist and architect*, Rome 1983.

EDUARD KEILIG (1827 - 1895) & THE BELGIAN LANDSCAPE ARCHITECTURE OF THE 19TH CENTURY

Katrien Hebbelinck
Artesis University College of Antwerp
katrien.hebbelinck@artesis.be
_

EDUARD KEILIG 1827-1895 (LE PETIT BLEU, 31 JULI 1895)

German designer Eduard Keilig is considered to be one of the most important representatives of the 19th century landscape style in Belgium. The same applies however to his colleagues and compatriots, Carl Heinrich Petersen and Louis Fuchs.[1] Belgian landscape architecture of the 19th century is characterised by a striking German presence. Yet from 1860, the French practice of Haussman, Alphand and Barillet

Deschamps becomes the international model in town planning and green design. The present research examines this German and French context from an individual case study. Its aim is to define the origin, characteristics and development of Keilig's work and to evaluate its position within the 19th century landscape architecture.

KEYWORDS

Landscape and garden design, 19th century, Belgium, Eduard Keilig

INTRODUCTION

Since 1992 the historical parks and gardens of Belgium have been systematically described.[2] The first results of these inventories reveal a booming period during the 19th century, with numerous new designs of both private and public parks. The 18th century aristocratic landscape style, until then reserved for private estates in the countryside, now reaches the city and its gentry. Fitting in with an emergent Belgian town planning, King Leopold II and the town administrations of Brussels, Antwerp, Ostend and Liège commission the layout of broad tree-lined avenues and public parks. Their inspirational model is the transformation of Paris under the guidance

1   See X. Duquenne, 'Der besondere Einfluss deutscher Gärtenkünstler in Belgien im 19. Jahrhundert', *Preussische Gärten in Europa*, Stiftung Preussische Schlösser und Gärten Berlin-Brandenburg, 2007, pp.252-255.

2   See N. de Harlez de Deulin, 'L'inventaire des parcs et jardins histo-riques de Wallonie', *Maison d'Hier et d'Aujourd'hui*, nr.122, 1999, pp.2-13 and C. De Maegd, R. Deneef, 'Kasteelparken en volkstuintjes historisch bekeken: De inventaris tuinen en parken in het Vlaams Gewest', in: *De Woonstede door de eeuwen heen*, nr.134, 2002, pp.10-25

TERKAMERENBOS, BRUSSELS (K. HEBBELINCK, 2004)

of Haussmann and Alphand. Yet the designers, working in Belgium at that time, appear to be German and might therefore have other models and traditions in mind.

The present research investigates this 19th century, Belgian landscape architecture from an individual case; in particular the works of German landscape and garden designer Eduard Keilig. Settled in Belgium since 1853, this designer has a remarkable number of public parks to his name. He is the author of the Brussels' Terkamerenbos, the town park of Antwerp and the Parc d'Avroy of Liège. For the Duke of Brabant and later king Leopold II, he works at the royal gardens of Tervuren and designs the public parks of Laeken and Ostend.

Until his death in 1895, Keilig combines these royal and urban design projects with an independent practice in private park and garden design.

Study into the history of Belgian landscape architecture, however, is scarce. The design of parks and gardens, as a separate science, with its own means and methods, is seldom put into words. Still less an individual design practice is subjected to analysis and evaluation. Keilig is said to be working in a so-called landscape style. But what does this mean? What links his work to the 18th century English cradle of this style, its German interpretation or the French topicality? Even an insight into the Belgian, 19th century context is so far

E. KEILIG, TOWN PARK, ANTWERP, 1868 (STADSARCHIEF ANTWERP)

lacking. Which designers are at hand and what kind of design-cases do they tackle? For which clients does Keilig work, and what are their resources and intentions?

The research examines Keilig's projects in relation to these (inter)national developments in style and context. Each designer operates in a historical perspective, works within a given context and reacts to current trends in his profession. Keilig's German origin and the French predominance in town planning and green design offer a broadened context, in which the significance of his career can be evaluated. The aim is therefore to define the characteristics and development of Keilig's work, as well as their origins and motives.

CONTENT AND SUBJECT

Up till now there has been no trace of Keilig's personal files. Before analysing this work, his career needs to be reconstructed, by means of both contemporary and recent literature and the remaining archives of his clients. A key document is Keilig's autobiography from 1866, mentioning his training and working experience in Germany, as well as his first

contacts and design commissions in Belgium.[3] In 1856 Keilig publishes both his five 'Lettres sur l'architecture des jardins' and his 'Observations sur la construction des petits jardins'.[4] These early texts give a valuable insight into the starting points of his designs. Testing these words to his practice will thus form the basis of the research.

These collected data provide an overview of projects, designed by Keilig, in Belgium, between the years 1853 and 1895. The research is mainly based on a close reading of a series of selected designs. Guided by Keilig's own words, we examine their plan, contemporary maps, representations and present state, in order to define their scale and type, the motive for their design, the origin and conditions of the site, and its relation to the surroundings. The main attention goes the layout of the design, its planting scheme, sightlines, circulation pattern, water display and architectural features.

To explain the thus detected characteristics of Keilig's work, the research investigates the variations and developments within the 19th century landscape architecture. Belgian literature on this matter is however limited and shows striking gaps in the areas of design and public green space. Even today, both context and comparison frameworks are mainly to be sought in German and French research. Only after a feedback of these findings to the Belgian context, can we evaluate Keilig's personal contribution to in the 19th century landscape architecture.

RESULTS AND DISCUSSION

In both the Netherlands and Belgium, the distribution of the 19th century landscape style is mainly attributed to German designers such as Michael, Zocher, Petersen, Weyhe, Gindra and Fuchs. At least up to 1860 they enjoy a particular

3   ARAB, Ministerie van Justitie, Naturalisaties, 1567: E. Keilig, 'biographie', 7.1.1866
4   E. Keilig, 'Lettres sur l'architecture des jardins', *Journal d'Anvers*, (I) nr.5, 20.2.1856, p.2, (II) nr.52 28.2.1856, p.2, (III) nr.66, 6.3.1856, p.2, (IV) nr.73, 6.3.1856, p.2, (V) nr.79, 19.3.1856, p.3 and E. Keilig, 'Observations sur la construction des petits jardins', *Journal d'horticulture pratique*, 13, (1855-1856), pp.244-250

appreciation, which will, probably for the last time, also apply to Keilig. As a designer, however, he proves to be self-educated. This might make him all the more dependent on professional advice and literature, available in Germany in the early 19th century. Therefore both Von Sckell's 'Beitrage zur Bildenden Gartenkunst für angehende Gartenkünstler und Gartenliebhaber',[5] and the translations of Loudon's 'Encyclopedia of Gardening' need to be taken into account.[6] Shortly after his arrival in Belgium Keilig gets acquainted with baron de Man de Lennick, owner of the castle of Bierbais and the host of the German landscape designer, Petersen. A professional relationship with the latter is likely to be of particular significance for a starting designer as Keilig. It might mean the confirmation of a German tradition in his work. To find out the possible characteristics of this tradition, the research examines the work and writings of Hirschfeld, Von Sckell, Pückler Muskau and Lenné.

Furthermore, a comparison should be made with both the Belgian context and the contemporary French practice. The designing contest for the Brussels' Terkamerenbos not only illustrates the Belgian approach to town planning and urban green space. Keilig's winning design and Barillet Deschamps' counterproposal also reveal the differences between the German Volksgarten and the French bourgeois citizen park. Soon, both clients and designers will respond to the leading role of the latter model. Six years later, Keilig's design for the city park of Antwerp shows a striking resemblance with the Parisian park of Buttes-Chaumont. Is he then putting his German tradition aside or does he create a Belgian compromise between both schools? If so, in what way does his work differ from his French or German contemporaries?

Keilig's name is mainly linked to royal and urban assignments. But he is also the designer of a remarkable range of private parks and gardens. It remains to be seen if Keilig approaches these designs differently; whether they show other characteristics or develop in a different way. The research into Keilig's works

thus contains all elements to provide a so far missing insight into the versatile context and practice of Belgian landscape architecture in the 19th century. ■

Ph.D Thesis Directors
Prof. Dr. Linda Van Santvoort (UGent),
Prof. Dr. Luc François (UGent)
Prof. Dr. ir.arch. Piet Lombaerde
Artesis University College of Antwerp

REFERENCES

Duquenne, X., *Le Bois de la Cambre*, Brussels, 1989.

Keilig, E., 'Lettres sur l'architecture des jardins', *Journal d'Anvers*, (I) nr.5, 20.2.1856, p.2, (II) nr.52 28.2.1856, p.2, (III) nr.66, 6.3.1856, p.2, (IV) nr.73, 6.3.1856, p.2, (V) nr.79, 19.3.1856, p.3.

Keilig, E., 'Observations sur la construction des petits jardins', *Journal d'horticulture pratique*, 13, (1855-1856), pp.244-250

Lombaerde, P., 'Eduard Keilig und der landschaftliche Park in Belgien', *Die Gartenkunst*, 1. Jahrgang, Heft 2/1989, pp.299-312.

Moens, J., 'Geschiedenis van het Stadspark Antwerpen', *Antwerpen*, (I) sept. 1981 nr.3 pp.157-164, (II) dec. 1981 nr.4 pp.189-192, (III) maart 1982 nr.1 pp.47-54.

---

5   F.L. Von Sckell, *Beitrage zur Bildenden Gartenkunst für angehende Gar-tenkünstler und Gartenliebhaber*, Munchen, 1825
6   J.C. Loudon, *Eine Encyclopädie des Gartenwesens*, Weimar, 1823-1826

ADS
19/20

FATHER AND SON VAN STEENBERGEN: A CENTURY OF ARCHITECTURAL PRACTICE IN ANTWERP

Pieter Brosens
Artesis University College of Antwerp
pieter.brosens@artesis.be
–

The proposed study is situated within a broader research on specific aspects of modernism in Antwerp. Little research has been done on the limiting conditions and various influences in which the regional modern form is rooted.

This research explores the work of two generations of architects: Eduard Van Steenbergen (1889-1952) and his son Edward (Van Steenbergen, 1925-2003). Throughout a formal evolution in their career, both architects accomplished a high standard of work which is representative for the time frame in which it arose.

The study focuses on gaining an insight into their actions and thoughts, taking into account social, political and cultural conditions. Besides a profound research on their work as architects, their role as teacher, publicist and member of numerous organisations needs to be considered. In this context, not only their contacts with other architects are important, but also the network of artists, politicians and commissioners needs to be uncovered.

Thorough archive studies, literature research and project analysis will reveal not only the personal choices and motives of both architects but also typical regional aspects of modernist architecture in Antwerp. The main research objective, using all these findings, is to outline some key issues regarding the changes within the architecture-culture and the architectural practice in Antwerp throughout the 20th century.

KEYWORDS

(Van) Steenbergen, Antwerp, modernism, postwar, (architectural) practice, art

INTRODUCTION

The examined period is marked by both World Wars. These encounters weighed heavily upon the social framework and the resulting political climate greatly influenced the thinking on architecture throughout the 20th century.[1] By researching two generations of architects in two different eras - both were in their twenties after the two World Wars some significant changes in the architecture-culture and architectural practice throughout the 20th century can be outlined. How they interpreted regional and/or (inter)national philosophies and how they materialized these during their careers needs to be explored, and also their interdisciplinary contacts and diverse collaborations by which their work could thrive must be looked at. These findings can reveal not only important aspects of local architectural and artistic inheritance, but also social and political points of interest related to culture in general.

In Antwerp not much systematic research on interbellum and

---

1   The period of research is defined by the start of Eduard Van Steenbergen's study at the Royal Academy of Fine Arts, at the beginning of the 20th century, and the death of his son Edward Van Steenbergen in 2003 and therefore nearly covers the whole of the 20th century.

UNITAS HOUSING ESTATE, DEURNE (1923)

RESIDENCE VAN DEN BERGHE, BORGERHOUT (1928) © VANDENBREEDEN J.
AND VANLAETHEM F., ART DECO EN MODERNISME IN BELGIË - ARCHITECTUUR
IN HET INTERBELLUM, TIELT, 1996.

post-war architecture has been conducted. Nevertheless, this architectural patrimony extends beyond its locality and needs to be put in a broader perspective, on a Belgian and even European scale. The present study contributes to filling up this lack of historical research and should contribute to a more general appreciation by the community by means of lectures, articles and exhibitions. General awareness of our patrimony is thus stimulated, and the knowledge and conservation of our built heritage more safeguarded.

The father, Eduard Van Steenbergen, and some of his projects are picked up in historical overviews but apart from various master thesis researches there are only a few articles and one book from 1955 on the architect and his work.[2] Research on this important Belgian modernist can fill the knowledge gap with reference to other protagonists of modernism that have been studied, such as Renaat Braem, Louis Herman De Koninck, Victor Bourgeois, etc. Edward Van Steenbergen, his son, was never much written about and therefore his work was nearly forgotten. Because of this limited appreciation their work begs not only a broader historical reflection but an updated writing as well.

CONTENT AND SUBJECT

Some basic aspects such as the layout of a scenario and the setting up of a timeline were started with. These documents are continuously adjusted and updated.

2   Van den Berghe V., *Eduard Van Steenbergen, bouwmeester en binnen-huiskunstenaar 1889-1952*, Antwerpen, 1955

Exhaustive archive research was conducted on the personal archives of both architects and most archives with project related material. The extensive corpus of personal and non-personal documents was located and listed in detailed inventories; most documents can be identified as primary sources. In addition, a great amount of bibliographic research was done. A literature study was conducted in order to evaluate and process primary and secondary sources.

ADS
19/20

Simultaneously, a network of people was built up: living witnesses, such as the widow of the son, colleagues, owners and occupants of buildings, etc. and experts in specific fields, such as archivists, historians and architects. Also the network of archives, libraries and institutions was laid out and consulted.

A general vision with goals was defined and a table of contents set up in a flexible and adjustable manner. The inventory system and the timeline, both displaying the paths and careers of both architects by means of a complete list of works and actions, were used as an underlying architectural framework. On that historical background different fields of research are implemented, such as art, urbanism, politics, the changing design practice and World War reconstruction. Within these fields different optional cases can be worked out that elaborate on important aspects of both architects' practice or the changing architectural practice in general. Some of the key subjects are considering crucial works and periods, not only in their careers but in general local architectural history as well. Current studies on the following cases are conducted: New monumentality in modernism, the Unitas Garden Suburb, the evolution in private housing design, interdisciplinary contacts, the role of the commissioner, etc. Papers on the first two subjects were already written and presented. Critical comments and adjusted insights are now worked upon.

RESIDENCE SPAENHOVEN, KEERBERGEN (1963) © LAUREYS D. (ED.), BOUWEN IN BEELD: DE COLLECTIE VAN HET ARCHITECTUURARCHIEF VAN DE PROVINCIE ANTWERPEN, TURNHOUT, 2004

Mainly the study is approached as an interpretive-historical research in combination with case studies.

RESULTS AND DISCUSSION

Many facts about father and son Van Steenbergen and the projects of both men are new and tell us a lot about modern and contemporary architects and how their profession changed throughout the 20th century. These diverse aspects, regarding context, complexity and approach, teach us about the adaptation and elaboration of the profession in general. Therefore, besides the uncovering of all sorts of specific data on the architects and their projects, a great deal can be learned from the evolution of their profession by placing these elements in the context of an evolving cultural, social and political Western society.

Because of the relevance of large amounts of data and the diversity of elements to be taken into account, a balanced and well thought out selection and interpretation of material needs to be undertaken. Regarding the problem statement, this process is a complex and a risk-bearing one. Still a lot of choices in that perspective must be made according to the line of vision to be taken and the definite vision to be outlined.

A lot of important research on interbellum and post-war architecture in Antwerp still needs to be conducted. Following to this study, it can be related to similar findings gathered here. ∎

Ph. D Thesis Directors:
Prof. dr. ir.arch. Piet Lombaerde
University of Antwerp
Artesis University College of Antwerp
Prof. dr. ir.arch. Yves Schoonjans
Sint-Lucas School of Architecture

REFERENCES

Bentein C. and Stynen H., 'Unitaswijk in Deurne (1923-1932)',
M&L, 1, 1982, 6, pp. 20-39.

Laureys D. (ed.), *Bouwen in beeld: de collectie van het*
Architectuurarchief van de Provincie Antwerpen, Turnhout, 2004.

Malliet A., 'Gebouwen van architect Eduard van Steenbergen uit
het interbellum', *M&L*, 12, 1993, 3, pp. 8-31.

Van Den Berghe V., *Eduard Van Steenbergen, bouwmeester en*
binnenhuiskunstenaar 1889-1952, Antwerpen, 1955.

Vandenbreeden J. and Vanlaethem F., *Art Deco en Modernisme in*
België - Architectuur in het Interbellum, Tielt, 1996.

Wilk C. (ed.), *Modernism: Designing a New World 1914-1939*,
London, 2006.

ROYAL ATHENEUM, DEURNE (1936) © VANDENBREEDEN J. AND VANLAETHEM F., ART DECO EN MODERNISME IN BELGIË - ARCHITECTUUR IN HET INTERBELLUM, TIELT, 1996.

LIFE SCIENCE BUILDING JANSSENS PHARMACEUTICA© PHARM, BEERSE (Z.J.) LAUREYS D. (ED.), BOUWEN IN BEELD: DE COLLECTIE VAN HET ARCHITECTUURARCHIEF VAN DE PROVINCIE ANTWERPEN, TURNHOUT, 2004

A MITIGATED MODERNISM: THE ARCHITECTURE OF DWELLING IN BELGIUM (1958-1973)

Eva Storgaard
Artesis University College of Antwerp
eva.storgaard@artesis.be

JEAN VAN DEN BOGAERDE. OWN HOUSE, 1966. (J. VANDEVELDE) (UIT: GEERT BEKAERT, HEDENDAAGSE ARCHITECTUUR IN BELGIË, LANNOO. TIELT 1995, P. 141)

A RESEARCH ON INNOVATIVE APPROACHES OF DWELLING ENVIRONMENTS BY LATE-MODERN ARCHITECTS AND INTERIOR ARCHITECTS

This research focuses on innovative approaches of dwelling environments brought to the fore by Belgian architects and interior architects in the period 1958-1973. These approaches can be qualified as 'mitigated modernism' and encompass as well a correction of the universalist tendencies of high modernism (1920s-1930s) as of the uniform character of post-war housing (1940s-1950s). Mitigated modernism is characterized by a sensibility for particular sites and contexts, specific building materials, local building practices and characteristic dwelling attitudes, as well as by an integrated method that simultaneously takes into account material, social and symbolic issues.

KEYWORDS

Architecture of Dwelling, Mitigated Modernism, 1960s, Belgium

INTRODUCTION

During the 1950s and 1960s international architectural culture as well as architectural practice in Belgium developed new visions and approaches of dwelling environments. These new tendencies in the late-modern period can be characterized as revisions or 'mitigations' of methods and themes brought forward by high modern architects during the 1920s and 1930s. This research holds a double hypothesis concerning this 'mitigated modernism'[1].

First, it holds that mitigated modernism implies a correction of the universalism (belief in universal solutions for housing problems) that was characteristic of the modern movement

1   See Geert Bekaert, *Hedendaagse Architectuur in België*, 'De laatsten van de modernen: de wacht wordt niet meer afgelost.', Tielt, 1995, pp. 77-141.

COVERS: DIEMER-LINDEBOOM ETAL BOUWEN, WONEN, LEVEN. (1966) AND F. PH. A. TELLEGEN. WONEN ALS LEVENSVRAAG. (1965)(EVA STORGAARD)

in architecture during the 1920s and 1930s. Instead, mitigated modernists favoured localism, focussing on the qualities and potential of particular sites and contexts, specific building materials, local building practices, characteristic dwelling attitudes, etc...

Second, the research holds that mitigated modernism encompassed a correction of the uniform character of 1950s housing –in which modernism was often reduced to mere rational building production. Mitigated modernists returned to the pluriform and integrated approaches that the architects of the modern movement had developed during the inter-bellum –focussing simultaneously on issues of building production, the social, the symbolic, etc...

Despite its innovative character, mitigated modernism and its new visions on dwelling environments disappeared rapidly from the Belgian architectural scene. From the seventies onwards there is barely a trace of these visions in architectural discourse. There are several reasons for this evolution. A first significant reason is the sudden rise of postmodernism in the architectural culture. From the mid 1970s post-modern ideas dominate the discourse of architecture in Belgium. As a

result the attention shifted from a mitigated modernism to an architecture where imagery gains major importance. Another reason has to be found outside the architectural culture. After the 1973 oil crisis and the subsequent period of insecurity, a neo-traditionalistic way of dwelling seems to conquer Belgium. The far most popular dwelling type becomes the *fermette*. This prototypical materialization of a 'retour aux champs' does not comply with modernist dwelling ideals.[2] The absence of common activities or groups among architects active during the late-modern period, can be regarded as a last reason for the fast disappearance of mitigated modernism. Unlike their high-modern predecessors and post-modern successors these architects generally operated alone and almost never managed to create a common attitude.

Because of all these reasons Belgian mitigated modernism of the 1950s and 1960s, especially the ideas concerning dwelling and interior, has fallen into oblivion. The architects from this period can be regarded as "a forgotten generation, who died a quiet death".[3] As a consequence, the work of these architects only scarcely appears in the history books of architecture and in the histories of dwelling culture in Belgium. As a result important contributions to the architecture of dwelling from this period never got adequate recognition. Likewise, the legacy from mitigated modernism has not been rated at its full value.

The present research investigates –from the perspective of architectural sciences– this legacy in late modern architectural culture. It wants to offer a critical examination of the contribution of mitigated modernism in Belgium during the period 1958-1973.

CONTENT AND SUBJECT

The subject of this research is situated at the field of encounter between dwelling culture (socio-cultural perspectives and patterns of dwelling) and architectural culture (visions and

2   See Bruno De Meulder, Jan Schreurs, Annabel Cock, Bruno Notte-boom, *Sleutelen aan het Belgische stadslandschap, in OASE #52*, 1999, pp. 78-113.
3   See Geert Bekaert, *Hedendaagse Architectuur in België*, 'De laatsten van de modernen: de wacht wordt niet meer afgelost.', Tielt, 1995, pp. 77-141.

JULES MOZIN. OWN HOUSE. 1961. (FROM: GEERT BEKAERT AND FRANCIS STRAUVEN, BOUWEN IN BELGIË 1945-1970, NATIONALE CONFEDERATIE VAN HET BOUWBEDRIJF, ANTWERP, 1971, P. 305)

approaches on the architecture of dwelling). This is reflected in the general research methodology. Hence, methodological approaches from the domain of the historical sciences (discourse analysis and oral history) will be combined with appropriate methods from the domain of the architectural sciences (plan analysis, typological and compositional analysis). This research project is structured in different phases that all have their methodological particularity.

A first phase consists of the development of a theoretical framework on dwelling. It encompasses a literature study (history, architectural history, architectural theory) and interviews with privileged witnesses (critics and theorists in architecture). The main purpose of this phase is to delineate a limited amount of 'common themes' on dwelling –themes that simultaneous were at stake in architectural discourse and in the socio-cultural debate (period 1958-1973).

In a second phase the 'common themes' –delineated in the first phase– are taken as a point of departure for the selection of exemplary architectural approaches and dwelling models (houses and housing projects). This first selection will be the basis for sub-hypotheses concerning mitigated modernism and its relation to dwelling culture.

In a third phase the sub-hypotheses will be tested through a detailed study of the exemplary dwelling models and architectural approaches. The theoretical framework, based on secondary sources, will be confronted with the study of primary sources such as architecture archives, buildings and interiors. This process will make it possible to sharpen or reformulate the sub-hypotheses and eventually adjust the choices of the different dwelling models.

Finally, a critical analysis of the sub-hypotheses will be made. This will result in general statements concerning the characteristics of mitigated modernism and its approach of dwelling culture.

RESULTS AND DISCUSSION

Lately several in-depth studies have been made on dwelling and dwelling culture in Belgium.[4] The majority of these investigations have mainly focused on the role and impact of socio-cultural organisations and actors, as well as on economic influences on dwelling culture. The contribution of architects through the development of dwelling models, dwelling schemes, houses and housing projects were often no explicit subject.

This research aims to complement these recent studies through a specific focus on architectural culture. It attempts to fill the missing link between the modern and the post-modern period in the history of Belgian architecture that was signalized by Geert Bekaert in his canonical work 'Hedendaagse Architectuur in België' (1995).

Moreover, until now only relatively few architects from this period are known. Thanks to a few monographies the works of Willy Van der Meeren, Peter Callebout, Lucien Engels, Jacques Dupuis, Albert Bontridder, Georges Baines, Pieter De Bruyne [5] ... were drawn into attention. Nevertheless, these architects represent only a top-layer of the generation of architects active in the fifties, sixties and the beginning of the seventies. This research wants to focus on the work of these well-known building masters and their personal correction of the modern, as well as on the projects of less known architects and their contribution to a mitigated modernism.

4   De Kooning, Mil, *Willy Van der Meeren*, in: Vlees en beton, nr 21-24, 1993; De Kooning, Mil, *Lucien Engels*, in: Vlees en beton, nr. 26-27, 1995; De Kooning, M.; Speliers, H., *Peter Callebout 1916-1970,* Vlees en Beton, nr. 35-36, Mechelen, 1998;
Cohen, Maurizio, Thomaes, Jan, *Jacques Dupuis, l'architecte*, Brussel, Editions La lettre Volée, 2000; Strauven, Francis, *Albert Bontridder, architect en dichter*, Brussel, Editions des Archives d'Architecture Moderne, 2005; Frampton, Kenneth, Strauven, Francis, Verpoest, Luc (et al.) *Georges Baines*, Gent, Ludion 2006; Storgaard, Eva, *Pieter De Bruyne. Meubels, Interieurs en Gebouwen 1955-1987*, Researchreport Artesis Hogeschool Antwerpen, Ontwerpwetenschappen, 2008.
5   Fredie Floré, *Lessen in Modern Wonen. Een architectuurhistorisch onderzoek naar de communicatie van modellen voor goed wonen in België 1945-1958*, doctoral thesis, UGent 2006, unpublished; Sofie De Caigny, *Bouwen aan een nieuwe thuis. Wooncultuur in Vlaanderen tijdens het Interbellum*, doctoral thesis, KULeuven 2008, unpublished; Els De Vos, *Hoe zouden wij graag wonen?*, doctoral thesis, KULeuven 2008, unpublished.

In a concluding chapter, the relevance of mitigated modernism and the dwelling models created in the period 1958- 1973 for the present architectural culture will be exemplified. ■

Ph.D Thesis Directors
Prof. Dr. Henk De Smaele (UA)
Prof. Arch. Christian Kieckens
Artesis University College of Antwerp

REFERENCES

Bekaert G., Strauven F., *Bouwen in België 1945-1970*, Brussel, Nationale Confederatie van het Bouwbedrijf,1971.

Bekaert G., *Hedendaagse Architectuur in België*, 'De laatsten van de modernen: de wacht wordt niet meer afgelost.', Tielt, 1995, pp. 77-141.

Van Herck K., Avermaete T. (eds.), *Wonen in Welvaart. Woningbouw en wooncultuur in Vlaanderen, 1948-1973*, Rotterdam, 010 Publishers, 2006.

ADS
19/20

THE CRITICAL ARCHITECTURE DIMENSION IN THE PLASTIC ARTS 'LA CITÉ TOURISTIQUE' BY CONGOLESE ARTIST PUME BYLEX

Koen Van Synghel
Artesis University College of Antwerp
koen.vansynghel@artesis.be
—

Language is the vehicle for intellectual labour. Disciplines such as philosophy and logic form the traditional basis of critical reflection. But 'images' in the hands of artists, especially visual artists, can work as critical tools. For images have the power to formulate an analytic and synthetic critic. This 'critic' can be implicit as explicit.

In the first place this doctorate is an investigation about the practises of contemporary artists and their modes of thinking into a language of material and form, of atmospheres and installations, of images and discourses. These practises reveal an alternative critic on architecture. To certain extend, one could say that artists in their work, formulate a more fundamental critic on architecture than architecture critics and historians. As artists are more free to connect their reflections on a broader interest in

Therefore the research is oriented by an anthropological point of view, to be able to see and connect architecture with a more general material culture. The research is based on a selection of multi-cultural artists, whose careers shows aspects of acculturation and whose work demonstrates a multi-disciplinary attitude.

Central figure is the Cherokee-American artist Jimmy Durham. As a human-rights activist he moved to Europe in the 70s. In his work (installations, books, films and video, drawings,...) he's not only critical about architecture but also about being critical as an attitude.

Durhams work will be confronted with other contemporary practises from different cultural backgrounds such as Europe, Africa, Asia,... In particular the work of Belgian artists like Thierry De Cordier and Jef Geys will be analysed.

De Cordier because of his particular position in building a mental refuge e.g. his statement 'Je n'ai rien a faire avec le XXième siècle', Jef Geys, for his interactive 1:1 model, built for the Biennale of Sao Paulo,... The African, Congolese artist Pume Bylex, who developed the idea for a Tourist City, the so called "Cité Touristique', an international, humanistic utopia, where the boundaries between religion and modernistic universalism are remodelled... The aim of the doctoral research is to reveal: critical methods and themes which discuss the fundaments of architectural conception, thinking. The hidden knowledge in the work of contemporary art can contribute to a more holistic thinking about architecture, and resource post-modern architecture.

KEYWORDS

Criticism – Foundation - Image – Language – Anthropology -

CONTENT

Language is the vehicle par excellence for intellectual work. Disciplines such as philosophy and logic contribute to critical reflection.

However, 'statues' in the hands of plastic artists also have the ability of expressing criticism both analytically as well as synthetically. The critical architecture dimension of the plastic arts can be extremely explicit or implicit in this process.

The aim of the doctoral research is to expose topics which question the foundations of architecture through the oeuvre of various contemporary plastic artists and thus to contribute to creating a better understanding of architecture.

The choice of the artists will take place on the basis of outspoken cultural embedding of their work. It is exactly this aspect of acculturation or the integration of various cultural backgrounds that forms an interesting angle to trace alternative concepts with regard to architecture which go against the rather sceptical acceptance of a generic architecture culture.

In order to prevent that architecture criticism becomes an autonomous, self-reflexive discipline, the research is therefore based on an anthropological substructure.

After all, architecture is part of a wider material and immaterial culture of which the plastic arts form an integral part.

This essay, as an extension of the research, explores the work of Bylex.

Bylex is the stage name of Congolese artist Francis Pume (born in 1968). Even though he is relatively unknown on the international art circuit, he has already exhibited several times in France and in Belgium. In 2003, he was selected for the group exhibition *Europe fantôme* in Brussels[1]. Nevertheless, Anyhow, Bylex has developed his own pictorial language. His objects, drawings, costumes, furniture, and scale models are recognisable at a glance and are part of one large single universe. Bylex is both a researcher, divine architect as well as a man of ideas. A true Demiurg who creates order in chaos. This is how he conducts virtually scientific research into the invisible laws and processes of the world. As an artist Bylex is not interested in the banal reality of Kinshasa. He prefers to focus on what lies behind the horizon or the visible and tangible. Thus, he penetrates into the mysteries of the invisible in order to create his own universe, with its own natural laws: a world in which the main focus is on perfection and harmony.

Especially for the exhibition *The World According to Bylex*[2], Bylex has created a scale model of *la Cité Touristique*. Bylex has been dreaming of this utopic city all his life. In his mind, this so-called tourist town has almost adopted a mythical place and it embodies his uncompromising striving for a better, universal world.

In the light of the history of architecture and town planning, and in particular utopic architecture, *La Cité Touristique* takes a special place. After all, Bylex's work has come into existence against the background of contemporary Kinshasa. A city in which architecture has achieved a nil grade[3]. Bylex's Kinshasa is that of Petro-Congo, a neighbourhood in the district of Masina. This is also sometimes referred to as *Chine populaire* because it is one of the most populated and extensive people's districts of Kinshasa. A dusty sandy road leads to a so-called *'parcelle', a* minuscule plot of land with a ditto house. This is Bylex's home. His home consists of a few small rooms which look out onto a small courtyard of a small house which he shares with other tenants. Petro-Congo regularly suffers powercuts. So the fan and the television remain off. The small lightbulb hanging from the ceiling does not emit any light. Bylex's house embodies the limitations and the frustrations of life in this big Central-African city. Bylex's work has to be viewed against this background of scarcity and lack, decay and hardship, limitation and obstruction, and his endeavours to overcome these limitations. Physically naturally, if possible, but also mentally, from an even more pressing inner need.

What interests Bylex is not the banal everyday reality. Or

1   Exhibitions in 1997 (Paris), 1999 (Bordeaux), 2000 (Lyons), 2003 (Brussels), 2004 (Roubaix), 2004-2006 (Düsseldorf, Paris, London, Tokyo), 2007 (Ostend). The Kinshasa edition of Revue Noire was published in 1996 (no. 21). Filip De Boeck met Bylex for the very first time in 2002, on the fringes of an earlier collaboration with photographer Marie-Françoise Plissart in Kinshasa. In 2003, Filip De Boeck invited Bylex to Brussels to take part in the exhibition *Europe fantôme* which he organised in conjunction with Jean-Pierre Jaquemin, and in 2007 Bylex again came to Belgium, this time for a work-related stay in Ostend, where the Cargo-workshop offered him a wider platform to express his ideas. Thanks to the collaboration with Stefaan Decostere, the inspiration behind Cargo, De Boeck and Van Synghel also travelled to Kinshasa in September 2006 to record an extensive interview with Bylex. These conversations also form part of the approach for *The World According to Bylex*.

2   Exhibition at the Koninklijke Vlaamse Schouwburg (Royal Flemish Opera) (30.05.2008-19.06.2008). Curators: anthropologist Filip De Boeck & architect Koen Van Synghel

3   Kinshasa, The imaginary City exhibition for the Biennale of Venice, see associated book Kinshasa, Tales of the Invisible City, Filip De Boeck, published by Ludion, Ghent, 2004.

as Filip de Boeck says it in 'The World According to Bylex', "not the *lived-in order* of daily life but instead a more mental order of things, a *thought-of order* which Lévi-Strauss would undoubtedly would have referred to as the *pensée sauvage*, that is to say, the underlying universal laws, the untamed thought processes (of *language*, of *competence*) which form the basis of the world before they are tamed by the social or cultural context in which they happen to be expressed." In the case of Bylex, this 'taming' begins in the context of Kinshasa , but he himself actually attributes little importance to this. Even though Kinshasa is undoubtedly present in his work, albeit in a more indirect way (also see *Cité Touristique*), this information in the eyes of Bylex is primarily a rather annoying coincidence. Bylex can just as well see himself live and work in New York, Paris or Tokyo. It does not actually matter 'where'." [4]

CITÉ TOURISTIQUE

The scale model of the *Cité Touristique* in polished plexiglass and shiny paper, at first glance looks like an oversimplified translation of a utopic belief in the possibility to extract oneself from this physical world, to leave the present city and to start afresh somewhere else. However, that 'starting again' is not absolute. It immediately ensures that Bylex's *Cité Touristique* takes an exceptional position between the tabula rasa utopias and the more context-bound visionary architecture. After all, this city is not just a visionary alternative for an existing city. Not for Kinshasa, nor for any world city for that matter. The *Cité Touristique* is in itself an analogous city. Not a utopia but a heterotopia in which the city in a type of densening of itself appears to be a refuge. A place where people can head to, to get new impressions and finally to reflect and to recharge one's batteries. In this sense the tourist city is not an Ideal City such as the renaissance architects imagined it as a reaction to the organically grown – *read* chaotic- medieval city. Not a perfect city. Not a city to live in. Strictly speaking, except for the hotels, Bylex does not even allow for any housing or living areas in his tourist city. Despite the royal title which Bylex confers upon it,

the central dome is not a Versailles or a Schönbrun. Actually, Bylex seems to come surprisingly close to the ideas of Paul Otlet (1868-1944) and his Mundaneum. A 'global' museum and the beginnings of a utopic city in which all the encyclopaedic knowledge about the world has been brought together. Bylex shares Otlet's humanist driving force in the way in which he wants to unite inspired knowledge and beauty and open it up to humanity. The form which Bylex uses to achieve this, is also reminiscent of Le Corbusier's design for the Mundaneum. Not literally, but exceptionally for him, Le Corbusier also designed a strong building, imbued with symbolism, in the form of a ziggurat. In contradiction to this age-old Assyrian temple typology which is related to the pyramids, for his Royal Dome Building Bylex adopts the later, Christian inspired central churches.

The entire architecture of the Tourist City is undeniably focused on this central dome building. A Spiritual Temple, the ecumenical, but also the temple for human beings without a God. This is where the 'tourist' is invited to, challenged, called to contemplate and reflect. This is where the tourist, in an aura of peace and quiet, is encouraged to mentally process the impressions gained in the hotels, the swimming pools, the artificial lawns, the shopping areas. Or let's say, to philosophise there. Bylex's wish is that the Royal Dome should appeal to the human ability to pose existential questions. In the assumption that this contemplation encourages human beings to become more intelligent and morally better. In this process, Bylex believes deeply in the power of architecture. You could actually state that Bylex nearly uses architecture as a 'belief system'[5]. He relies on the details and the interior design of the buildings, the perfection of the architecture, to convey his humanist message in an empathetic manner.

An integral part of Bylex's *Cité Touristique* is therefore the manner in which he implements the notion of 'tourism'. All

4 Filip De Boeck & Koen Van Synghel, in The World According to Bylex, published by Koninklijke Vlaamse Schouwburg, Brussels, 2008, P. 5.

5 In this context it is important to refer to Jimmy Durham. The oeuvre of this American artist of Cherokee origin, forms the central focus of this doctoral research. Durham is extremely critical with respect to Western, and in particular European architecture, which he reproaches to be acting as a belief system, in which the right of existence of the architecture seems to be founded on convincing, indoctrinating or making people believe something, such as the cathedrals in the sense of Guy Debord's "Spectacle" to make people believe something.

in all, the facilities which he plans are fairly limited. You can hardly refer to the hotels and the shopping centre as unique centres of attraction for a tourist city. The radical choice for artificial and perfectly shiny material, and especially the lack of any natural vegetation - Bylex talks neither of trees or plants but he does talk of *synthetic lawns*, artificial grass in yellow, blue, orange – distance the city radically from the usual artificial tourist paradises and resorts. This is where Bylex's saying is very appropriate: 'Why not this'. It is exactly by homing in on synthetic perfection that Bylex wants people to experience a particular frame of mind, a type of shock, which should lead to a catharsis in the visitor. This takes us perhaps too far but in his city Bylex unknowingly adopts the principles of the Situationists, who at the end of the 1950's, pleaded against boredom and the utilitarianism in architecture and town planning. One of the protagonists, Gilles Ivain, then thought up city scenes imbued with symbolism and magical places, which just like the Royal Dome, should stimulate imagination. Ivain's absurd sounding language and ideas "the Our Lady Mary Zoo", transparent concrete", the "Foreigners' Hotel", "The Wild Street"[6] resound in Bylex's language and universe. Bylex's *Cité Touristique* is naturally closely related to the work of another Situationist, the Dutchman Constant and his New Babylon project. Constant's city utopia was founded on the premise that in modern society machines would take over the production of goods from human beings, and would thus create a sea of leisure time. Constant therefore lifted the city, with its road infrastructure and so on, so that the landscape except for a few supporting pillars, would be freed for the Homo Ludens. Bylex does not take the city transformation that far. His city is not focused on a utopic human being who is freed from work by a very sophisticated technological society. Bylex's *Cité Touristique* will stand beside the existing city and take place in a sort of limbo between hell or reality and the heaven of the ideal city.

In this respect, Bylex differentiates himself from his spiritual contemporaries who believe in the possibility of a general 'clearing of the decks'. The belief in a modernistic city, the breaking away from the past, time and the history of the current city, he naturally shares with other visionaries and utopians in Kinshasa. But exactly by focusing on the tourist component of the city, which turns his city into a city *next to* a city, he turns in another direction than the in the meantime internationally renowned Bodys Isek Kingelez, who makes futuristic, ultramodern alternative Kinshasas out of paper maché and coloured paper. Mirroring Le Corbusier's *Ville radieuse*, Kingelez's largest city scale model is entitled *Ville fantôme*, a modernistic utopia which responds to the paradigms of the industrial metropolis. Here Kingelez's city vision shows itself as a utopia in overdrive, a Kinshasa for the third millennium, a future paradise packed with architectural deliria, luxurious skyscrapers and eccentric government buildings. Between the airport and the city, the Bridge of Death separates the good and the bad souls. The latter are denied access to the city, and they disappear into a ravine which forms the dividing line between the city and the rest of the world.[7] In the scale models of a city created by both Kingelez and Bylex, the model for a better society is situated in a spatial and temporal 'elsewhere'. The real anchoring in the here and now of the city, such as it exists today, is therefore non-existing, or in the case of the *Cité Touristique*, marginal. The utopia therefore remains captured in the atmosphere of pure possibility, or the ideal. It represents possibilities which cannot be materialised, and which can therefore not hold great power for fundamental change. Nevertheless, the *Cité Touristique* represents a world which appeals to the imagination. Not the power of imagination. But instead an appeal to real freedom, i.e. free thinking. A universal thinking which is not conditioned by location or culture but where human beings are the main focus. In a nutshell, a humanistic appeal.

Ph.D Thesis Directors
*Promotor: Prof. Filip De Boeck, KULeuven
(former professor at the UA, Antwerpen)
Co-Promotor: Architect Christiaan Kieckens,
Hogeschool Artesis, Antwerpen*

6   Also see Gilles Ivain "Formulaire pour un urbanisme nouveau", Internationale Situationiste (1958).

7   Also see André Magnin 2003, Interview the Bodys Isek Kingelez. In: *Bodys Isek Kingelez*. Brussels: La Médiatine.

PREVENTING CULTURAL PROPERTY DESTRUCTION DURING ARMED CONFLICT

Sigrid Van der Auwera
Artesis University College of Antwerp
sigrid.vanderauwera@artesis.be

During the twentieth century a lot of prevention measures to protect cultural property from looting and destruction during armed conflict were designed. Despite these measures, extensive looting and wanton destruction during armed conflicts had increased by the end of the century. Hence, this research aims at inventorying and evaluating these measures in order to develop an enhanced prevention strategy. These goals will be reached by analysing primary and secondary literature, by interviewing experts and policy makers and by analysing current cases. Until now, this research shows that, while a significant amount of prevention measures exist on different levels, implementation, coordination and cooperation is lacking.

KEYWORDS

Cultural property
Protection of monuments and sites
Armed conflict

INTRODUCTION

Whereas the world was confronted with some recent examples of destruction of cultural property during armed conflict[1], many other severe instances received less or no media attention[2]. The protection of cultural property during armed conflict is, however, important for more than one reason.

1   E.g. Buddha's of Bamiyan, Mostar Bridge, Iraqi National Museum
2   E.g. extensive looting in Colombia, the Lebanon, Israel/Palestine, Kosovo, Bosnia, etc.
3   C.K. Savich, *The Systematic Destruction of Orthodox Christian Churches and Cemeteries in Kosovo-Metohija and Macedonia*, 2002, available on http://www.kosovo.net/default1.html

RUINS OF THE SERBIAN ORTHODOX CATHEDRAL OF THE HOLY TRINITY IN DJAKOVICA[3]

Firstly, there are obviously cultural-historical considerations (preservation and management of heritage, importance of *in situ* conservation, etc.). Further, the protection of cultural property has economic implications: cultural property can, via cultural tourism, play a role in the rehabilitation after the conflict. Moreover, the protection of cultural property can contribute to conflict resolution and peacekeeping, because intentional destruction of cultural property plays more than once a key-role in the conflict as such.

The term 'cultural property' is used here because international law on the protection of cultural heritage during armed conflict

ADS
19/20

uses this term too. It includes material cultural heritage, such as built heritage, archaeological sites and cultural artefacts.

We could distinguish three ways of cultural property destruction during armed conflict: collateral damage, intentional destruction and looting.

When destruction of cultural property was not intentional and not foreseeable, it can be considered collateral damage. Mostly, however, destruction is intentional. Opposing parties try to hit each other psychologically by demolishing property that symbolises the identity of the opposing group. On the other hand, embargoes, lack of financial resources and inadequate methods to protect sites and monuments benefit the looting of museums and sites. In a globalized world, especially the problem of intentional destruction and looting seems to have increased in the last decades.

This happened in spite of the fact that, during the twentieth century, ever more prevention measures to tackle the looting and wanton destruction of cultural sites and monuments were developed.

Hence, the main research question that we will consider is: how can we explain that in spite of the significant amount of prevention measures designed by the international community during the twentieth century, the extent of wanton destruction of cultural heritage had actually increased by the end of that century?
The aim of this research will consequently be to inventory and evaluate prevention measures in order to develop an enhanced prevention strategy.

In recent years, a great deal of attention has already been devoted to destruction of cultural property during armed conflict. Existing research is, however, mostly discipline-specific and considers either a certain aspect of prevention or a case that describes the phenomenon as such. In particular, numerous studies have focused on the relevant international

law[4] or the archaeological implications[5]. While destruction also involves other disciplines, like political sciences, military sciences, economics and especially preservation studies, a more holistic approach seems to be absent. Moreover, especially the aspect of prevention has been relatively ignored. Hence, this research considers the prevention strategy in an integral framework. To assure the multidisciplinary character, it is carried out at the University College of Antwerp, Department of Design Sciences in the framework of the Master Program Conservation of Monuments and Sites, in cooperation with the University of Antwerp, Department of International Politics and Department of Law and the University of Ghent, Department of Languages and Cultures of the Near East.

CONTENT AND SUBJECT

In order to reach those aims, first an inventory and a typology will be designed bottom-up, starting from the different prevention measures, by analysing primary and secondary literature and by interviewing experts. The typology will then be translated to a 'model strategy'. Finally, this will be evaluated top-down on the basis of contemporary cases.

RESULTS AND DISCUSSION

While inventorying the prevention measures, we concluded that the measures can be grouped into five types of providers, namely law, politics, civil society, the heritage sector and private heritage administrators and the military:
The relevant international humanitarian law has been developing since 1500 and reached a culmination point in 1954 with the adoption of the Convention on the protection of cultural property during armed conflict and a First Protocol. The Balkan War urged the adoption of a Second Protocol in 1999. The International Criminal Court for the Former Yugoslavia recently pronounced some judgments that punished war

4   i.a. K. Chamberlain, *War and cultural heritage. An analysis of the 1954 Convention for the protection of cultural property in the event of armed conflict and its two protocols*, Leicester, 2004., P. O'Keefe, *The Protection of cultural property during armed conflict*, Cambridge, 2006.
5   i.a. M. Gibson, 'From the prevention measures to fact finding missions', *Museum International*, 55, 2003, pp. 108-118., N. Brodie, J. Doole, P. Watson, *Stealing history. The illicit trade in cultural material*, Cambridge, 2000.

crimes against cultural property and qualified some of them even as crimes against humanity.

These international juridical sources stem from political decision-making. Other measures are also developed at this level. In past times, some states established special services to cope with the protection of cultural property during armed conflict. Evacuation plans and plans for the building of refuges are mostly designed on a political level. In Croatia, for instance, the Ministry of Culture decided to move cultural objects to safer places and to protect monuments and sites by technical measures (wooden structures, sandbags, etc.). Moreover, international organisations, like UNESCO and ICCROM are engaged in the protection of cultural property during armed conflict. Lastly, diplomatic actions can be undertaken to spare cultural property.

Civil society tries through advocacy to act upon policy and to raise awareness on the topic. By the end of the twentieth century, one could witness a proliferation of such movements[6] and research institutes and individual researchers engaged increasingly in the study of the phenomenon.

The heritage sector and private heritage administrators can make preparations in peacetime by drawing risk preparedness programs and by adequate inventorying. When an armed conflict breaks out, they have to manage the evacuation or the *in situ* safeguarding.

Lastly, the armed forces play a role in the protection of cultural heritage during armed conflict. They mostly are the only persons that can actively operate in a precarious safety situation. They can guard sites and monuments, organise convoys to bring objects to safer places, prevent attacks on cultural property, etc. Besides, the forces themselves must refrain from any act of hostility against and from the military use of cultural property. Moreover, in the past, some states established special services within their armed forces to protect cultural property. [7]

In spite of all these measures, the problem of looting and intentional destruction of cultural property seems to have increased in the last decades. Consequently, we think that it is not in the amount of measures that the strategy is lacking. We acknowledged, however, that not all of the inventoried measures are used during a certain conflict. It appears that these measures always have to be reinvented during a certain conflict and that coordination, cooperation and interaction between the different actors is lacking.

Moreover, this seems to coincide with the occurrence of a new type of warfare, the so-called 'new wars', 'low intensity conflicts', 'small wars', etc.[8] Such wars are frequently identity-based and a common history plays a role in the process of political mobilization. Cultural property destruction is then used as a weapon of psychological warfare. The heritage of the other party has to be erased in order to render the territory ethnically homogeneous. In other words, the destruction of cultural property becomes part of the conflicts as such. Among others, we ascertained this phenomenon in Bosnia, Croatia, Kosovo and Israel/Palestine.

In addition, these conflicts are ever more privatised. The monopoly of the state on violence has decreased. The strife is therefore no longer solely financed by the state parties. The insurgents have to search for revenues themselves. Therefore they engage in criminal activities.[9] The looting of museum and sites and the illicit trade in antiquities can, in some instances, be interpreted in this regard. In Iraq, Afghanistan and Colombia, proof supporting this theory was found.[10]

6   i.a. ICBS, ICOM, ICOMOS, IFLA, ICA, ICRC, WMF, WATCH, SAFE, AÏNA, SPACH, PMDA, etc.
7   Probably the most famous were the American Monuments, Fine Arts and Archives (MFFA)-officers in the Second World War.

8   i.a. M. Kaldor, *New and old wars. Organized violence in a global era*, Cambridge., 1999, E. Conteh-Morgan, *Collective political violence. An introduction to the theories and cases of violent conflicts*, New york, 2004.
9   i.a. M. Kaldor, *New and old wars. Organized violence in a global era*, Cambridge., 1999, I. Bannon, P. Collier, *Natural Resources and violent conflict. Options and actions*, Washington D.C., 2003.
10 N. Brodie, J. Doole, P. Watson, *Stealing history. The illicit trade in cultural material*, Cambridge, 2000., J. Goodhand, H. Atmar, *Afghanistan: the Challenge for peace in Central and South Asia*, 2002, www.euconflict. org, M. Bogdanos, 'The casualities of war: the truth about the Iraq Museum', *American Journal of Archaeology*, 2005, July, pp. 477-529.

ADS
19/20

CONCLUSION

This research analyzes why the prevention strategy to tackle the destruction of cultural property during armed conflict lacks and how it could be enhanced. Until today, although still preliminary, our research indicates that it is not in the amount of measures that the strategy is lacking, but that is rather due to:

- the *ad hoc* character of the initiatives and a lack of lessons-learned;
- a lack of coordination, cooperation and interaction between the different levels where prevention measures are initiated;
- a lack of adjustment to the way in which contemporary conflicts appear and to the motives and profiles of the culprits. ∎

Ph. D Thesis Directors
Prof. Dr. Annick Schramme
University of Antwerp
Assoc. Prof. ir.arch. André De Naeyer
Artesis University College of Antwerp

ADS
19/20

A RESEARCH INTO THE BODY OF THEORY OF INTERIOR ARCHITECTURE IN FLANDERS, FRAMED IN AN INTERNATIONAL CONTEXT

Inge Somers
Artesis University College of Antwerp
inge.somers@artesis.be
–

The relationship between the development of a body of theory and the development of interior design/architecture as an independent discipline in Flanders is the subject of the present research project. [1]

This hypothetical relationship between interior architecture as an emerging discipline parallel to the formation – due to an apparent lack – of a body of theory formed the basic assumption for Stanley Abercrombie's reference work, 'A Philosophy of Interior Design' (1991). In the preface, James Stewart Polshek, dean of the School of Architecture and Planning at Columbia University, mentioned that interior design could not be considered a true profession because it lacked a body of theory. This is a striking claim at the end of the 20th century, considering that professionals in the interior area already appeared at the end of the 19th century and that independent interior design/architecture training programs started up shortly after the second world war.

In Flanders there is also an additional tension because of the limited social recognition and legitimation of the discipline of interior architecture as it is not a protected profession unlike architecture. At the same time, the development or/and the recognition of a proper body of theory of interior design/architecture is indeed a rather recent phenomenon. [2] This project will examine this development and frame the results in an international context, considering the fact that the Anglo-American theoretical debate is well-known for a longer tradition.

KEYWORDS

Interior architecture, body of theory, Flanders, professionalism.

INTRODUCTION

'Interiors is an evolving yet slippery discipline. Among all designed artefacts, interiors themselves are uniquely ephemeral and difficult to define. The practice of interiors is relatively unregulated. The history of interiors is patchy and contested. The theoretical basis of interiors is largely unexplored in comparison to those of other disciplines. How, therefore, might we speculate about the role, validity and purpose of interiors in the twenty-first century?' [3]

---

1   The terms 'interior design' and 'interior architecture' will be used as interchangeably in this text, while in the Anglo-American literature the difference is not so clearly made as in Flanders.

2   See Paula Baxter, 'Thirthy Years of Growth in the Literature of Interior Design', Journal of Design History, vol.4.nr.4, 1991, pp.241-250.

3   See introduction of publication 'Thinking inside the Box', a reader in interiors for the 21st century, ed. by Interiors Forum Scotland, 2007, p.11.

85

ADS
19/20

This text summarizes briefly the basic concerns for starting up this present research. Being an interior architect myself, working in the field of interior architecture for about 20 years and being part of the educational team of the independent interior architectural training program in Antwerp, this continuing lack of clarity has been the motive for a profound investigation.

A preliminary inquiry during the last year brought the focus on the development of a theoretic basis. If the boundaries of interiors are so hard to define as well as the field of action of interior design/architecture and of the interior designer/architect, maybe the reason could be found in the lack of a sincere theoretical debate. When the debate within the discipline – not to mention a desirable consensus – is missing, it is hard to achieve recognition and legitimation. That brings us back to the statement of James Stewart Polshek (supra). The main issue that will be investigated is the following: is the rather belated development of a body of theory the underlying reason for the tension between the emancipatory dynamic of the discipline at the one hand ('implicating the wish to establish a more intellectually respected and more cerebral educational process and practice') and it's limited social recognition and legitimation on the other hand. [4] And is this a typical Flemish or an international phenomenon?

CONTENT AND SUBJECT

The following main objectives will form the frame-work of this investigation.

The first objective is creating an insight in the origin of the training program in Antwerp. We look at the *zeitgeist* and theoretical ideas that underlay this initial curriculum. The results of this investigation will be compared to the theoretical influences on the other two master programs in Flanders, which only followed later.

The second focus is on the vacuum in the theoretical debate within interior design / architecture and the relation between the establishment of theory within interior architecture and architecture. This part of the research requires a study of the international theoretical debate, whereby the work of reference of Stanley Abercrombie form the basic assumption. By studying the different nuances within the recent theoretical self-reflection of the interior discipline, I hope to be able to sharpen the concepts, in an attempt to make the discipline less 'slippery'. This part of the inquiry creates also the opportunity to spit out the obstacles which arose in the evolution of the discipline and in the development of a proper body of theory and which were created by the conflation of the interior with the domestic, the amateur and the feminine. The breaking up of these historical associations leads to new opportunities for interior design/interior architecture.

These new evolutions and the benefit of the interaction between theory and training programs on the one hand and theory and practice on the other hand are the subject of the third objective. Recent national and international developments within the discipline will be mapped and this part of the research will try to expose the importance of the theoretical debate for the evolution of the discipline. Theoretical reflection is a condition for a discipline to evolve as it enriches both its education and its practice.

The last objective is working out a case study in collaboration with the Department of Sociology at the University of Antwerp. The intention of this case study is to put into practice the established theoretical framework and to underline the possibilities of academic interdisciplinary collaboration for interior architecture.

RESULTS AND DISCUSSION

This Ph.D. project starts in January 2009. The preliminary inquiry during 2008 already provided some insights on certain aspect of the objectives, mentioned above.

1. Taking into account the numerous conferences organized worldwide that deal with interior design/architecture and research, and the growing academic publications about the discipline the last ten/fifteen years, we can state that

4   See 'Thinking inside the Box', a reader in interiors for the 21st century, ed. by Interiors Forum Scotland 2007, 2007, 'Consensus or Confusion' by Shashi Caan, p.49.

interior design/architecture is in evolution.[5] There is a vivid and growing international theoretical debate going on, boosted by the academical switch of the discipline partly caused by the dynamics of the Bologna Declaration of 1999. There is also the concern for the accreditation of the training programs. This project will help to orientate and contextualize the internal debate on curriculum and research.

2. Academic research on interiors and on the discipline of interior architecture has been hampered during the 20th century by the tendency to conflate the interior, the domestic, the amateur and the feminine. These conflations formed the obstacle for the study of the interior to be considered of any academic value. The domestic interior has been the realm of women from the end of the 19th century till late 20th century, and therefore it was not for till late in the 20th century considered a subject for investigation and theoretical reflection.

3. A first reading of the literature affirms that although the theoretical debate is still in development the lack of clarity and consensus concerning the identity of interior design/architecture has not been resolved yet. The interior has never been the exclusive field of action of interior designers/architects. Also decorators and architects deal with interiors. The same can be said about the theoretical discourse of interiors. During the 20th century it has been pursued as part of the architectural theoretical discourse. There is mingling of the three disciplines - decoration, architecture and interior design/architecture - in practice and in theoretical discourse. One cannot escape the impression that interior design/architecture is still considered as the light version of architecture. ■

Ph.D Thesis Directors
Prof. Dr. Luc Goossens (UA)
Prof. Dr. Koenraad Van Cleempoel (UHasselt)
Prof. ir.ar. Tijl Eyckerman
Artesis University College of Antwerp

REFERENCES

Abercrombie,S., *Century of Interior Design 1900-2000: The Designers, the Products and the Profession.* Rizzoli International Publications, New York, 2003.

Abercrombie, S., *A Philosophy of Interior Design.* Westview Press, US, 1991.

Cieraad, I., Hertzberger, H., M., Vuyk, K., *Van binnen uit. Interieurarchitectuur in ontwikkeling.* Uitgeverij Thoth, Bussem, NL 2001.

Journal of Design History, special issue, *Professionalizing Interior Design 1870- 1970,* volume 21, number 1, 2008.

Peressult, L.B., Forino, I., Postiglione, G., Scullica, F., *Places & Themes of Interiors, Contemporary Research Worldwide.* Interiors Studies Franco Angeli, Milaan, 2008.

Rice, C., *The Emergence of the Interior.* Routledge, London and New York, 2007

Rendell, J., Penner, B. and Borden, I. (eds), *Gender Space Architecture.* Routledge, London and New York, 2000.

Taylor, M. en Preston, J., *Intimus, Interior Design Theory Reader.* Wiley Academy, West Sussex, England, 2006.

---

5 Some important conferences af the last years: IFI Round Table Conference (Singapore, 2006), The Professionalisation of Decoration, Design and the Modern Interior (London, 2006), Thinking inside the Box (Edingburgh, 2007), First Professional Interior Design Conference (Dubai, 2007), Places and Themes of Interiors (Milan, 2008), Interior Tools Interior Tactics (Edingburgh 2008)
For the publications see references and article P.Baxter (note 2).

ACTIVITIES

LECTURES

- Assoc. Prof. Jan CORREMANS presented a paper 'Basic Skills in the Study of Form - teaching experiment' on the 5th September 2008 during the 'Engineering and Product Design Education Conference 2008', Barcelona, Spain, 04 - 05 September 2008.
- Assoc. Prof. ir.arch. André DE NAEYER delivered a lecture on 'Conservation and change of historic buildings' at the Interdisciplinary Training School Conference 'Science and Technology for the cultural heritage', Genoa, 10-15/09/ 2007. At the EAAE-ENHSA (European Association for Architectural Education - European Network of Heads of Schools of Architecture) -workshop Univ. di Genova (It.) 18- 20 October 2007 "Teaching conservation and restoration of built heritage", he was a keynote speaker and held a lecture on:"How do we teach conservation and restoration of built heritage".
- Assoc. Prof. ir.arch. Johan DE WALSCHE presented a paper 'Teaching architecture: a strategy of (re)organizing and reinterpretation" at the EAAE-Conference "Teaching and experimenting with architectural design – advances in technology-changes in pedagogy", Lisbon, 3-5 May 2007. He held a lecture on "The portfolio-concept as a Tool for Assessing Competences in Architectural Education" at the Tempus Reformae II meeting at Belgrade, 8-9 February 2008.
- Full Prof. ir.arch. Richard FOQUÉ delivered a lecture *"Towards a Competences Based Qualifications Framework"* at the Ss.Cyril and Methodius University, Faculty of Architecture, Skopje, Macedonia, 06.10.2007. He presented a paper on *"A Strategy for a Competences Based Qualifications Framework"* at the Joint Meeting of ACSA Administrators and ENHSA (Association of Collegiate Schools of Architecture - European Network of Heads of Schools of Architecture), University of Minnesota, Minneapolis, USA, 31.10.2007. He held a lecture *"Toward Competency-based Education in Architecture: A Dialogue with America"* at the University of Belgrade, Faculty of Architecture, Serbia, 08.02.2008. At the Department of Architecture of the Pontifical Catholic University of Lima-Peru, he held a lecture *"A Strategy for Implementing Competences Based Architectural Education"*, 14.02.2008. He presented also a paper *"The Portfolio Concept as a Tool for Assessing Competences in Architectural Education"* at the same University, 15.02.2008. At the Research-Day of the Artesis University College Antwerp, he delivered a paper on *"Ontwerpen en Onderzoeken"*, 08.10.2008.
- PhD-student Saskia GABRIEL delivered a lecture on 'Assessing Daylight and Fire Safety in the Integrated Architectural Design of Atria', Climacademy course 4, 6-11 May 2008, Pamporovo, Bulgaria.
- Ass. Prof. Dirk LAPORTE presented a paper on 'Herbestemming van kerken, geslaagde en minder geslaagde voorbeelden' at the symposium 'In ander licht. Toekomstperspectieven voor religieus erfgoed in Vlaanderen', Abbey of Bruges, 23 February 2008.
- Ass. Prof. Maria LEUS delivered a lecture on 'Cultural biography as an instrument for revitalization' Congres: Living and walking in cities, Universities Parma / Brescia, 19 –20 June 2008; 'Cultural tourism a challenge for revitalisation', at the Cost Congres, Paphos Cyprus, 01-02 September 2008; 'The emotion of the place', at the ICOMOS' International Scientific Symposium 'Re-thinking the spirit of place Quebec', Quebec, 27 September –05 October 2008.
- Prof. Dr. ir.arch. Piet LOMBAERDE held a lecture on *'Two Controversial statues in the Public space: Alva in Antwerp and Erasmus in Rotterdam'*, at the International Colloquium 'Renaissance Sculpture of the Low Countries from the Century of Jacques Du Broeucq, c.1505-1585', Mons, 07-

10 March 2008. He held a lecture 'Wy a new book on the former Jesuit Church of Antwerp?', on the occasion of the publication of the book 'Innovation and Experience during the Early Baroque in the Southern Netherlands. The case of the Jesuit Church in Antwerp' (*Architectura Moderna* Series n°6, Brepols Publishers), Antwerp, St.Carolus Borromeus Church and Museum Rockox House, 18 April 2008.

He delivered a lecture on 'Exporting Urban Models: The Low Countries and Northern Germany, Schleswig-Holstein and Denmark', during the International Colloquium *The Low Countries at the Crossroads. The Influence of Netherlandish Architecture in Europe 1480-1680*", KU Leuven, Kasteel van Arenberg, Heverlee, 30-31 October 2008.

- Associate Prof. Marc MUYLLE presented the paper "Digital Verification of Innovative 17th Century Illumination Theories used in the Design of Flemish Baroque Churches "at the DACH 2007 conference, January 12th to 14th, on 'Digital Applications in Cultural Heritage', in the historical city of Tainan, Taiwan (Republic of China). He joined the workshop "Imag(in)ing architecture: Iconography in nineteenth century architectural historical publications", Leuven, June 1st.

- PhD-student Ann PISMAN held a lecture on 'Uitdagingen voor de ruimtelijke ordening in Vlaanderen', during a Congress organised by 'Steunpunt Ruimte en Wonen ', Brussels, 26 July 2008. She joined the ACSP-AESOP Congress Chicago 'Bridging the divide: celebrating the city', Chicago, 6/7/2008-11/7/2008; and from 15/6/2008-18/6/2008 she participated at the AESOP PhD workshop Jotunheimen, Norway.

- PhD-student Nathalie POPPE delivered a lecture on 'De optica van François de Aguilón en haar impact op de bouw van de St.-Carolus Borromeuskerk te Antwerpen', at the 20th Symposium on: "Antwerpen, groeipool van de wetenschappen', University of Antwerp, 23 May 2008. She presented her doctoral research work at the Joint Doctoral Seminar, Leuven, 30 April 2008.

- PhD-student Sigrid VAN DER AUWERA took part at the 5th International Conference on Science and Technology in Archaeology and Conservation, Granada, 7-12 July 2007,

with a paper on: 'Destruction of tangible cultural heritage in conflict and post conflict situations. The need of an interdisciplinary approach to meet future challenges.' She joined the 10th International Civil-Military Relations Seminar, Vienna, 06-09 November 2007; where she presented a paper on: 'Cultural awareness and the protection of cultural heritage in peacekeeping'. She participated at the International Conference "Protecting Cultural Heritage in Times of Armed Conflict. Second Protocol to the Hague Convention – How to Make it Work?", Tallinn, 7-8 February, 2008. She presented a lecture on 'Commemorating the First World War and Flanders Fields: a short overview on the commemoration in 25 states' at the International Seminaries on "Remembering the Great War: a worldwide perspective", Flemish Community, Ieper, 6 June 2008

- Associate Professor Karine VAN DOORSSELAER held a paper on 'Biocomposieten in de voertuigindustrie', at a conference organized by *Flanders Drive* in collaboration with Centexbel, Ghent, 12 September 2008.

- Ass. Prof. Dirk Van Gogh presented a paper on:" 'T.H.E.-method', a Visualised Assessment Tool Used for Integrated Product Development", during the Congress 'International Association of Societies of Design Research, (IASDR07), The Hong Kong Polytechnic University, Hung How, Kowloon, 12/11/2007 – 15/11/2007; he held a lecture on 'Multidisciplinary Approach of Furniture Designing', during the Congress 'International furniture Conference and Exhibition in Malaysia', 27/07/2008 – 01/08/2008.

- Prof. Dr. Thierry VANELSLANDER held together with Hilde Meersman and Tom Pauwels a lecture on '*The Relation between Port Competition and Hinterland Connections*' at the International Conference 'The Role of Seaports as a Link between Inland and Maritime Transport', United Nations Economic Commission for Europe (UNECE), Piraeus, Greece, 17-18/9/2008.

- Associate Prof. Hendrik VAN GEEL held a lecture on 'Competence based learning in Urban Design and Spatial Planning, University of Belgrade, Faculty of Architecture, 08-10 February 2008.

- PhD-student Elli VERHULST held a lecture on *Duurzaam ontwerpen in het onderwijs*', at a infomation event 'Ecochic', treating sustainability in the building process and designing, organized by the Centrum Duurzaam Bouwen, Heusden-Zolder. 20 November 2007.

PUBLICATIONS

- DE GRANDE G. and BAELUS G., 'Bridging the Gap between product design and product engineering, E&PE 2008: New perspectives in design education
- Proceedings of the 10th engineering an product design education international conference, Barcelona Spain – Vol 1- p447
- DE NAEYER A., (ed.), Handboek Onderhoud, Renovatie en Restauratie , Ed. Kluwer, Mechelen (since 1998), part 36 (July 2008) + 35 (mei 2008) + 34 (Feb.2008) + 33 (oct. 2007).
- DE NAEYER A. 'Integration of built heritage in regional development projects – a reflection on technical points of restoration and reuse of heritage', in: G. ALLAERT (ed.): 'Cultural heritage and regional development', Ghent, 2007, pp. 29-32
- FOQUE R., 'A Strategy for a Competences Based Qualifications Framework', in: *Proceedings of the Joint Meeting of ACSA Administrators and ENHSA*, University of Minneapolis, Minnesota, 2007.
- FOQUE R., 'A Strategy for Implementing Competences Based Architectural Education', in: C. Spiridonidis (ed.), *Proceedings of the Conference on Competences Based Curricula Reforms* Pontifical Catholic University of Peru, Department of Architecture, Lima, 2008.
- FOQUE R., 'Towards Competency-based Education in Architecture: A Dialogue with America', in: V.P. KOROBAR and J. SILJANOSKA (eds.), *Reformae II, (Ss.Cyril and Methodius University, Faculty of Architecture)*, Skopje, 2008.
- FOQUE R., 'The Chania Meetings, A Decade of Building a European Higher Architectural Education Area', in: C. SPIRIDONIDIS and M. VOYATZAKI (eds.), *Transactions of Architectural Education*, (nr. 41, EAAE), Leuven, 2008.
- FOQUE R., *Notes on the Design Studio as a Competence Generating Tool*', in: V.P. KOROBAR and J. SILJANOSKA (eds.), *Reformae II, (Ss.Cyril and Methodius University, Faculty of Architecture)*, Skopje, 2008.
- FOQUE R. and APELT H., 'The Winning Smile of Taste', in:*Proceedings of the 3rd EAAE-ENHSA Subnetwork Workshop on Architectural Theory*, Universidade Lusofane de Humanidades e Tecnologias, Lisboa, 2008.
- JACOBY A., 'Success factors in New Product Development: How do they apply to company characteristics of academic spin-offs?', in: S. H. DE CLEYN, A. JACOBY and J. BRAET, *Proceedings of the R&D Management Conference*, Canada, 17-20 June 2008.
- LAPORTE D., 'De voormalige stadsfeestzaal van Antwerpen, Geschiedenis', in: *ICOMOS (International Council of Monuments and Sites) Contact Vlaanderen-Brussel*, 20, 2007,1, pp. 8-15.
- LAPORTE, D., 'Ons Huis en Bond Moyson Gent', 'Woning Van Hoecke-Dessel Gent', 'Hoekwoning Verniers Gent', 'Woning Crommen Gent, Directeurswoning, kantoren en werkhuizen Beauval Gent', 'Feestlokaal Vooruit Gent', ''De Cirk' te Gent' in: *Art nouveau, Van Old England tot het Paleis Stoclet, (De Standaard Architectuurbibliotheek, 1000 jaar architectuur in België, Vol.6)*, Tielt, 2008, pp. 42-43, 76-77, 82-83, 96-97, 106-107, 110-111, 114-115.
- LAPORTE, D., 'Nederlands Toneel Gent', 'Museum voor Schone Kunsten Gent', in: *Neostijlen en eclecticisme, Van Justitiepaleis tot de Cogels-Osylei, (De Standaard Architectuurbibliotheek, 1000 jaar architectuur in België, Vol.7)*, Tielt, 2008, pp. 96-97, 106-109.
- LAPORTE, D., 'Hotel Vanden Meersche Gent', 'Universitaire aula Gent' in: *Rococo en neoclassicisme, Van de Munt tot Fort Napoleon, (De Standaard Architectuurbibliotheek, 1000 jaar architectuur in België, Vol. 8)*, Tielt, 2008, pp. 50-51, 104-107.
- LAPORTE, D.,'Tweede Korenmetershuis Gent', in: *Renaissance en barok, Van Plantin-Moretus tot het Rubenshuis, (De Standaard Architectuurbibliotheek, 1000 jaar architectuur in België, Vol. 9)*, Tielt, 2008, pp.106-107.
- LAPORTE, D., 'Gravensteen Gent', 'Korenstapelhuis Graslei

Gent', 'Ruïne Sint-Baafsabdij Gent', 'Sint-Jacobskerk Gent', 'Kleine Sikkel Gent', 'Sint-Niklaaskerk Gent', 'Bijloke Gent', 'Het Pand, Gent', 'Sint-Baafskathedraal Gent', 'Belfort Gent', 'Gildehuis der Vrije Schippers', in: *Romaans en gotiek, Van het Gravensteen tot het stadhuis van Leuven*, (*De Standaard Architectuurbibliotheek, 1000 jaar architectuur in België, Vol.10*), Tielt, 2008, pp. 20-21, 26-27, 34-35, 42-43, 44-45, 46-47, 66-67, 68-69, 72-73, 80-81, 116-117.

- LOMBAERDE P., 'Stedenbouw en verkeer', in : *Antwerpen in de 20ste eeuw. Van Belle Epoque tot Golden Sixties*, Antwerp, 2008, pp.210-234.

- LOMBAERDE P., 'Questionnement sur le statut de l'architecte au début du XVIIIe siècle: l'Exemple des Van Baurscheit à Anvers', in : J. TOUSSAINT (ed.), *Actes du Colloque : Autour de Bayar/Le Roy*, Namur, 2008, pp.181-196.

- LOMBAERDE P., 'Teaching Theoretical Courses of Urban Design', in: J. SILJANOSKA and V. KOROBAR (eds.), *Reformae. Feforming Architectural Education in the CARDS Countries*, Skopje, 2006, pp.81-91.

- LOMBAERDE P., 'Koninklijke Sint-Hubertusgalerijen, Brussel', 'Wintertuin, Brussel', 'Thermenpaleis, Spa', 'Leopold II-galerij, Spa', in: *Neostijlen en Eclecticisme. Van het Justitiepaleis tot de Cogels Osylei*, Tielt, 2008, pp. 22-23, 46-47, 48-49 en 62-63.

- LOMBAERDE P. (ed.*), Innovation and Experience in the Early Baroque Architecture in the Southern Netherlands. The Case of the Jesuit Church in Antwerp*, Antwerp, 2008.

- MUYLLE M. (ed.), *Proceeding of the 08 Conference Architecture 'in computero' Integrating Methods and Techniques on: Architecture*, Antwerp, 2008.

- PISMAN A., 'Focus on housing demands in spatial planning', in: *8ᵉ Ugent-FirW*), Ghent, 2007, p. 66.

- PISMAN A., 'Onderzoek naar verbanden tussen woonvoorkeuren, leefmilieus en ruimtelijke planning in Vlaanderen', in: *Symposium Proceedings Mooi bedacht, nuttig toegepast*, Brussels, 2007, p.81.

- PISMAN A., *Landelijk of stedelijk wonen in Vlaanderen: een bewuste en een vrije keuze?. Discussienota woonregieboek Zuid-West-Vlaanderen*, s.l., 2007.

- POPPE N., 'Architectural Lighting in Baroque Churches. A Case Study of Basic Design Research', in:: J. SILJANOSKA and V. KOROBAR (eds.), *Reformae. Feforming Architectural Education in the CARDS Countries*, Skopje, 2006, pp.246-50.

- POPPE N., 'The phenomenon of day-light in the interior of the Antwerp Jesuit Church: towards a new interpretation', in: P. LOMBAERDE (ed.), *Innovation and experience in the early Baroque in the Southern Netherlands. The Case of the Jesuit Church in Antwerp*, Turnhout, 2008, pp.141-153.

- SPITAELS E., 'Architectuur', in: Genootschap voor Antwerpse geschiedenis (ed.), *Antwerpen in de 20ste eeuw, van Belle Epoque tot Golden Sixties*, Brasschaat, 2008, pp.234-256.

- VAN DER AUWERA, S., SCHRAMME, A. and JEURISSEN, R., 'Erfgoed en onderwijs in dialoog' in: *School en Samenleving*, Vol. 16, 2007, pp. 91-112.

- VAN DER AUWERA, S. (2007), 'Erfgoededucatie in het Vlaamse onderwijs' in: *CULTUUR + EDUCATIE 19*, pp. 8-27.

- VAN DER AUWERA, S. (2008), ''New wars' and heritage destruction' in *Interpreting the past. The future of heritage. Changing visions, attitudes and contexts in the 21ˢᵗ Century. Selected Papers from the Third Annual Ename International Colloquium. Monasterium PoortAckere, Ghent, Belgium, 21-24 March 2007, Brussel: Province of East-Flanders/Flemish Heritage Institute (VIOE)/Ename Center for Public Archaeology and Heritage Presentation*, p. 237-249

- VANELSLANDER Th., MEERSMAN H. and VAN DE VOORDE E., (2008), 'The Air Transport Sector after 2010: A Modified Market and Ownership Structure', *European Journal of Transport and Infrastructure Research*, 8, 2008, 2, pp. 71-90.

AWARDS AND NOMINATIONS

- Assoc. Prof. ir.arch. Johan DE WALSCHE was nominated for two prizes of the Flemish Master Builder: July 2007 "Project for a basic school in Zemst"; 2008: " Project of a basic school in Bocholt'.

- Assoc. Prof. arch. Christian KIECKENS was selected for the *J. Stübbenpark Duinbergen* competition (Germany), 2008 and for the 'In Flanders Fields Museum Ypres' Project 2008.

EXHIBITIONS AND PROJECTS

- Ass. Prof. Elie D'hondt participated at the exhibition 'Experimenteel Atelier Academie Temse', Exhibition DACCA Temse, June 2008.
- Ass. Prof. arch. Dirk JANSSEN organised an individual exhibition in the Gallery ZINKWIT in Utrecht; 17 February – 17 April 2007.
- Ass. Prof. arch. Elsa SPITAELS is member of the scientific committee of the Exhibition 'Renaat Braem' to be organised in *DeSingel*, Antwerp, Autumn 2010.
- Ass. Prof. Dirk VAN GOGH participated at the exhibition on conceptual design "Vormgevers@work '08", organised in 'De Zaal', Ghent, 29/02/2008 - 23/03/2008. This exhibition was organised in collaboration with the University College Ghent, the *Stichting Bruynseraede De Witte* and *VZW Kunsten Site*. He participated also at the exhibition "No Man's Land, between art and design", organised by the Verbeke Foundation, Kemzeke, 15/12/2007-04/05/2008.

ERASMUS

- Assoc. Prof. Lieven BONNAERENS participated at the workshop "Design and development methodology' (European Project Semester EPS), UPV-Etsid, Universidad Politécnica de Valencia, Spain, 28 September to 4 October 2007.
- Assoc. Prof.ir.arch. André DE NAEYER supervised ERASMUS-student Jonas VAN LOOVEREN during his research work at the Univ.degli Studi di Genova – Scuola di Specializzazione in restauro dei monumenti.(1rst semester 2007-2008).
- Ass. Prof. Dirk JANSSEN participated at the ERASMUS-exchange programme for professors and organised seminars at the Unversidad Politecnica de Valencia, April and June 2007.

OTHER ACADEMIC & RESEARCH ACTIVITIES

- Prof. Chris BAELUS participated at the Congress E&PE 2008: *New perspectives in design education*, (10th engineering and product design education international conference), Universitat politecnica de Catalunya, Barcelona, 4 –

September 2008.

- Assoc. Prof. Lieven BONNAERENS participated at the EPS-Provider (European Project Semester) meeting, with a lecture on 'Presentation of the Product Development Program as a potential EPS provider', Vilanova i la Geltrú (Spain), 3 - 4 December 2007.
- Assoc. Prof. ir.arch. André DE NAEYER was the Belgian delegate for the Domain Committee "Transport and Urban Development" (E.U. COST Program (European Cooperation in the field of Scientific and Technical Research), Brussels. He was delegated by the Vlaamse Gemeenschap for the E.U.COST Action C27: "Sustainable development policies for minor deprived urban communities"; and for E.U.COST Action TU0701: "Improving the quality of suburban building stocks". He was member of the Scientific Committee of the International workshop "Touches of Renaissance", (R. del Bianco Foundation), Florence, 13-20 November 2008. He is a permanent member of the doctoral commission of the Collegio Docenti 'Dottorato di Ricerca in Beni Culturali', Politecnico di Torino, Italy.
- Assoc. Prof. ir.arch. Johan DE WALSCHE participated at the EAAE-Congress "Teaching and experimenting with architectural design – advances in technology-changes in pedagogy", Lisboa, 3-4-5 May 2007. He joined the Tempus Reformae II meeting, Belgrade, 8- 9 February 2008; and the Tempus Reformae II Project, Ochrid, Macedonia, 13-15 June 2008. He participated at the 11th Meeting of Heads of European Schools of Architecture "New Responsibilities of Schools of Architecture, preparing Graduates for a Sustainable Career in Architecture", EAAE, ENHSA, Hania, 6-10 September 2008.
- Full Prof.ir.arch. Richard FOQUÉ was Visiting Distinguished Professor at the Carnegie Mellon University, School of Architecture Pittsburgh, USA. He was Academic Advisor at the Middle East Technical University, Ankara Turkey; Academic Advisor of the Tempus Projects Reformae 1 and 2, on Recognition of Architectural Degrees in CARDS Countries based on Competences and Learning Outcomes.
- Ass.Prof. arch. Christian KIECKENS organized the ADSL-

workshop week for the Higher Institute of Architectural Sciences January 2008, Antwerp.

- Ass. Prof. Dirk LAPORTE was member of the Jury of the Herman Delaunois Prize (*Koninklijke Vereniging voor Natuur- en Stedenschoon*), October 2007.

- Assoc. Prof. Maria LEUS participated at different international congresses: International Congress "Urban Heritage" –Vilnius Lithouwen, 24/09/2007-26/09/2007; International Colloquium "Middeleeuwse baksteenarchitectuur", Ten Bogaerde Koksijde, 24/10/2007-27/10/2007; International Congress Minor Deprived Communities, Sundsvall (Sweden), 12/03/2008-16/03/2008; International Symposium 'paradoxes and appearances' Copenhagen, 08/06/2008-12/06/2008; International Congress: The Urban Project TU Delft, 04/06/2008-07/06/2008.

- Prof. Dr.ir.arch. Piet LOMBAERDE was designated as expert of UNESCO for the nomination of 14 Vauban sites in France on the World Heritage List 2008. He participated at the International Congress 'Oeuvrer en atelier sous l'Ancien Régime: les ateliers au XVIe siècle', Toulouse, Université Toulouse II-Le Mirail, 4 December 2008.

- Assoc. Prof. Marc Muylle organized the eCAADe 08 Conference Architecture 'in computero' Integrating Methods and Techniques.

- PhD-student Ann PISMAN participated at the Conference 'Best practice in the presentation and market-oriented valorization of cultural heritage as an instrument of regional development', Ghent, 27/11/2007.

- PhD-student Nathalie POPPE participated at the exhibition on 2007 old books and prints in the Library of the former Royal Academy of Arts, Antwerp, 2007. She wrote a short personal impression on the book: *Architectura pars altera de opticens tractans*, by G.C. Bodenehr, c. 1700.

- Assoc. Prof.dr. Karine Van DOORSSELAER organized the course 'Milieugerichte Productontwikkeling' for the 'Postacademische opleiding Intergrale Productontwikkeling', KUL-Campus Kortrijk, 1 February 2008.

- Assoc. Prof. Hendrik VAN GEEL coordinated the Young Planners Workshop at the 43ste ISoCaRP congres (International Society of City and Regional Planners), Antwerp, Department of Design Sciences, 14 - 19 September 2007.

- Ph.D-student Ellie VERHULST was selected for and participated at the International Doctoral Educational Program *The Case Study: Fieldwork and Qualitative Methodology as a Research Strategy*. DOME, University of Aarhus, Denmark, 7-12 September 2008.

- PhD-student Elli VERHULST was research member of the project '*Ronny en Susy, een project rond duurzame innovatie roadmapping*', in collaboration with the Design Office smidESIGN.